Jane E Sprole
from her friend
The Author.

on Steel by John Sartain Phil.

Allen F. Gardiner

SELF-SACRIFICE,

OR

THE PIONEERS OF FUEGIA.

COMPILED FOR THE BOARD OF PUBLICATION,

BY SARAH A. MYERS.

PHILADELPHIA:
PRESBYTERIAN BOARD OF PUBLICATION,
No. 821 CHESTNUT STREET.

W. W. HARDING, STEREOTYPER.

CONTENTS.

INTRODUCTION.

FIRMNESS and constancy of purpose that withstands all solicitations, and in spite of all dangers goes on straight to its object, is very often sublime. The resolution of St. Paul in going to Jerusalem, where he had the firmest conviction he should undergo every species of danger and persecution, is a beautiful instance of the moral sublime, and there is something exceedingly majestic in the steadiness with which the great apostle of the Gentiles points out the single object of his life, and in the unquenchable courage with which he walks towards it. He says, "What mean ye to weep and to break my heart? I am ready, not to be bound only, but to die at Jerusalem, for the name of Jesus." "I know that ye all, among whom I have preached the kingdom of God, shall see my face no more." "Ye yourselves know that these hands have ministered to my necessities." "The Holy Ghost witnesseth in every city, that bonds and afflictions abide me; but none of these things move me, neither count I my life dear to myself, so that I might finish my course with joy, and the ministry which I have received, to testify the gospel of the grace of God."

Many have been called heroes, conquerors, conquered captains or soldiers who fought bravely; but then was it not for their own interest or advancement? In like manner, kings, legislators, the founders and destroyers of empires, might display enlarged views, profound policy, or an extensive acquaintance with men or with the times; they might evince genius and prudence, but they did not exhibit virtue—for the word *virtue* implies self-devotion or self-sacrifice. They sought but their own glory, and sacrificed, not themselves to others, but others to themselves, and thus their great deeds savoured rather of egotism than of virtue. The martyrs of the early ages, who were persecuted for the sake of religion, and sacrificed themselves for what they believed to be the truth, were true heroes; and there are many of later days—missionaries of the cross—who, following in their footsteps, go forth boldly, to break the bread of life to those who are perishing for want of spiritual food.

We do not, however, include within our list of selfish heroes, those who have gone forth on scientific explorations; for these, too, are missions intended to benefit man; and the gallant and benevolent Franklin, and his men, whose melancholy fate forms so sad a parallel to that of the martyrs whose history we are about to relate, deserve a more conspicuous niche in the temple of fame than did those, who to serve their own ambitious purposes, overran and conquered kingdoms. They found the cruelest of deaths, surrounded by the desolations of the polar regions, and their bones for months lay bleaching upon the icy wastes—the snows their only winding sheet; the cry of the arctic sea-birds their only requiem. Our own gallant Kane, too, not less a martyr than they, though permitted by a wise Providence to return, but only to find a grave in his native land, is not less a hero, since his errand, too, was in the cause of humanity. Their names are emblazoned on the page of history; their epitaphs are written in the hearts of their countrymen.

These martyrs in the cause of science have had the sympathy of an admiring world; while those seven devoted men who went forth in the zeal of high duty, taking their lives in their hands, to bear the news of salvation to savage men, and face the terrors of a waste volcanic region, where nature was as niggard of her bounty as on the icy wastes of the arctic region, are known, comparatively, to but few. Nevertheless, their "record is in heaven," and although we cannot fathom the mysteries of the Providence which permitted so sad a termination to their efforts in this glorious cause of bearing the gospel light to those who are sitting in darkness, their memory shall not perish, for are not their names written in the Lamb's book of life?

The following account of the life, labours, sufferings, and death of these martyrs to missionary zeal has been chiefly compiled from the Memoirs of Allen F. Gardiner, Commander, R. N., by the Rev. J. W. Marsh, and of Surgeon Richard Williams, by the Rev. Dr. Hamilton.

SELF-SACRIFICE,

OR

THE PIONEERS OF FUEGIA.

CHAPTER I.

PATAGONIA.

FROM the earliest days of Church history, we find that a missionary spirit has been abroad; the mantle of the apostles has fallen on many, and the command, "Go ye and preach my gospel, and teach all nations, baptizing them in the name of the Father, and of the Son, and of the Holy Ghost," has been obeyed. Devoted men, believing in the assurance, "Lo, I am with you always, even unto the end of the world," have gone forth boldly and erected the standard of the cross, on the remotest shores of savage Africa, as well as on the desolate ice plains of the polar lands. But whilst the gospel was preached to savage negroes, and the semi-savage nations of the far north were converted; whilst "Ethiopia stretched out her hands to God," and the islands of the great oceans waited for and rejoiced in the glad tidings brought by the heralds of the cross, Patagonia, the most remote portion of South America, had been neglected. Of considerable length, extending from the republic of La Plata to the straits of Magellan, it includes all the continent south of Fort Maullin in latitude 41° 43′, its greatest length from north to south being 1300 miles, its breadth from Cape Lobos to the Andes, 700 miles. The range of sea coast on the Atlantic side is 1100 miles; on the Pacific, 700. Buenos Ayres is its northern boundary; its eastern shore is washed by the waters of the Atlantic; the Pacific and Araucania lie in the west, and the straits of Magellan divide it from the island of Terra del Fuego on the south.

The whole of the eastern coast is dreary and barren; a tree, even in the neighbourhood of large rivers, is rarely seen to refresh the eye with its verdure or give shelter with its shadow; the vast and seemingly interminable Pampas, waste and desolate as the steppes of northern Europe, shut in by the Andes on the west, and on whose surface herds of wild horses or flocks of ostriches assemble, stretch their immense lengths from the Atlantic boundary to boundary. The climate is healthy; but the soil is most unproductive, because it seldom rains in this region. On the western coast, along which the range of the Cordilleras stretch, the heavens are rarely clear; the sky is canopied with thick clouds, and a steady fog increases the dreary aspect which nature has chosen to assume in this most uninviting region. The Europeans, that adventurous race of men who have forced their way to the remotest portions of the earth, have never been able to effect a settlement here. Nature, mostly generous, has been too niggard of her bounty to tempt even those who voluntarily seek toil and danger in savage lands and still more savage seas, to seek and find a home in Patagonia. The wild and hungry shores of the northern parts possess but few objects of curiosity; and unimproving, such as they now are, the same aspect is now presented that appeared before the eyes of early voyagers, and which has long since been so well described. Perpetual winds, rocky cliffs, driving currents, a coast utterly destitute of vegetable productions, save the deep and interminable forests that fringe the Andes on the western coast, a thinly scattered race of human inhabitants, existing upon the shell-fish as it takes refuge, or is thrown by the action of the waves in the interstices of the rocks, form no inviting prospect for the adventurous. A few whaling vessels have touched there, remaining just long enough on the coast to seek the sea elephant which is found in the Antarctic Ocean, to prepare train oil from the blubber, and remark the desolation that has prevented man from settling there.

Even the missionary spirit, the sublime endeavour which induces the devoted followers of Christ to forsake home and friends, and go to the most inhospitable regions to preach the word of life to those who sit in darkness and the shadow of death, had, before the period of which we are now writing, been comparatively but little awakened in behalf of the savage nations of the far south; no man seemed to care for their souls. Some English ships sent out in 1827 on an adventurous survey in the dangerous straits of Magellan, and which at first was no more successful in the attempt at scientific discovery than was the expedition to find out the north-western passage by the lamented Franklin, brought such accounts of the natives as to awaken, first, some curiosity, and afterwards interest, as to whether their condition might not be improved, and themselves elevated in the scale of humanity, by preaching the gospel among them, and teaching them the arts of civilization. The Patagonians, or South American Indians, were described as being in the main friendly, but exceedingly savage. It was said that, like the Arabs, the Indian tribes roaming between the Cordilleras and the Atlantic were wild and free: their hand was against every man, and every man's hand against them. Their uncommon stature has been mentioned; indeed, Commodore Byron speaks of them as a race of giants. Some travelers assert that none of this race are under six feet; but this is most probably an exaggeration.

The Patagonians are a strong and well built

race, muscular and robust. Their faces are round, somewhat flat, their heads somewhat large in proportion, their eyes are very lively, and they have teeth extremely fine and white. Like other Indian tribes they have long straight hair, which is very black, and which they wear tied up behind, bound many times round the head, and fastened in the crown. A few of them wear beards, but they were neither large nor bushy. Their complexion is copper colour, that of the women being considerably lighter than the men. Their clothing is very scanty. The men wear a single coat or garment, made of guanaco skin, with the hair on the outside. This thrown around the body, and without sleeves, is confined at the waist by a leathern girdle. The women wear nothing on the head, but have their long hair plaited in two large tresses, which hang down on each side. They have the same kind of mantle as the men, which they fasten before with a brass skewer or pin. A short apron, woven of dyed yarn and striped longitudinally, is worn over the mantle, and reaches a little below the knee. The men paint their faces in stripes or lines, sometimes red and sometimes black; like all savages, they are fond of ornament, and adorn themselves with sky-coloured beads around their necks and wrists.

The women have ear-rings or pendants of square brass plates, and strings of beads or necklaces, made from shells or the bones of small animals. When they ride, they use a straw hat of a broad conical figure. Both sexes wear boots or stockings made of the skins of horses' legs: these, the hoof not being removed when flayed, are dried, softened with grease, and made pliant by wringing, and, put on without shaping or sewing, tend greatly to increase the likeness these races bear to the brute rather than the human creation.

Rude and savage as their own rocky and stern river coasts, they are nevertheless not without ingenuity. Their weapons of offence are made with some skill. They consist of spears, bows and arrows, and slings, the latter of which they use with such precision as nearly to equal in effect an ordinary musket. Besides these they have the Patagonian *bolas*—a chain shot of formidable character. It consists of two round stones covered with leather, and fastened to the two ends of a string about eight feet long. One stone is held in the hand, whilst the other is whirled round the head until it acquires sufficient velocity, and then both are hurled at the object. Should it strike the legs of an ostrich or guanaco, it instantly twists tightly around them, and holds the creature in fetters until the huntsman comes up. Like all other tribes of wandering savages, they live almost entirely upon the spoils of the chase. The flesh of the wild lama, horse, and ostrich forms the staple of their food; however they are by no means dainty, but eat almost everything, and have been known to make a meal of tallow candles with seeming relish, swallowing the cotton wicks and all.

That "man really wants but little" is fully exemplified in the life of a Patagonian. His horse is his earthly all, treasured more than wife and children, and his dwelling is of the simplest and rudest construction; fitted rather for the lair of savage animals than an abode for human beings. It may perhaps be well for the edification of those of our readers who know little of these remote regions, to give some account of their temporary habitations, than which nothing more wretched can be conceived.

When in the course of their nomadic wanderings it is deemed advisable to stop, as soon as a family arrive at a convenient place, the first care of the women, who are the only workers, is to build a house. For this purpose they cut down twenty or thirty trees, and arranging them in a circle, at certain distances apart, the area being fifteen feet, with the narrow ends resting on each other, like the sheaves in a shock of corn, some pliant twigs keep the ends of the branches together, which being bent form a centre at the top. It is rendered comfortably warm and air-tight by a covering of boughs and seal-skins on the windward side, leaving one entrance toward the sea and another toward the forest. They kindle a fire in the centre, around which they huddle together night and day in stormy weather, little incommoded by the smoke which cannot possibly escape, there being no aperture at the top, but through the doorway, which, being so low, renders its egress almost impossible. The furnishing of the interior corresponds with the rude outside. A few skins on which they sleep, an old bag, a few cups, which made of skins serve them for drinking, some small stones on which they roast their meat, and a bundle of pointed poles which they use in drying skins, constitute the whole of their movables. The Patagonians occupy a very low rank in the scale of humanity. They are represented as being brave, warlike, and friendly to strangers, but also lazy, thievish, treacherous, and embruted in ignorance.

Their ideas of a Superior Being are extremely vague and dark, although all the Patagonian tribes believe in two superior principles, the one good and the other evil.

They believe that their good deities made the world, and that they first created the Indians in their caves, gave them the lance, the bow and arrows to fight and hunt with, and then turned them out to shift for themselves. They imagine that the deities of the Spaniards did the same by them, but that, instead of lances, bows, &c., they gave them guns and swords. They suppose that when the beasts, birds, and lesser animals were created, those of the more nimble kind came immediately out of their caves, but that the horned cattle being the last, the Indians were so frightened at the sight of them that they stopped up the entrance of their caves with great stones: which is the reason they assign why they had no horned cattle in their country till the Spaniards brought them over, who, more wisely, had let them come out of their caves.

From the evil principle, they say, proceed the great number of demons, which they suppose are constantly wandering about the earth, and to whom they attribute every evil that befalls man or beast. They are full believers in sorcery and witchcraft, and each of their wizards is supposed to have two of these demons in constant attendance, who enable them to foretell future events, to discover what is passing at a great distance, and to cure the sick, by combating or appeasing the other demons, who torment them. They believe that the souls of their wizards after death become demons. Their worship is entirely directed to the evil being, except in some particular ceremonies made use of in reference to the dead.

The profession of the wizards, notwithstanding the respect that is mostly paid to them, is very dangerous; for it often happens when an Indian chief dies, that some of the wizards are killed, especially if they have had any dispute with the deceased just before his death.

In cases of epidemic disorders, when great numbers are carried off, the wizards often suffer. At one time, when the small-pox had almost entirely destroyed one of the tribes, the cacique, Cangapol, ordered all the wizards to be put to death, believing that by that means the distemper, which was attributed to the sorcerers and their demons, would cease. The wizards are of both sexes, but all wear female apparel. They are chosen to this office when they are children; are clothed very early in the dress, and presented with the drum and rattles belonging to the profession they are to follow.

The burials of their dead, and the superstitious reverence paid to their memory, are attended with great ceremony; varying, however, in the different tribes. With some, when an Indian dies a woman is immediately chosen to make a skeleton of his body; the entrails and flesh are burned, and the bones are buried till the remaining flesh is wholly consumed, or until they are removed, which must be within a year after the interment, but is sometimes within two months, to the burial place of their ancestors. But the true Patagonians place the bones on high, upon canes and twigs woven together, to dry and whiten in the sun and rain. During the time that the ceremony of making the skeleton lasts, some of the tribe, covered with long mantles and their faces blackened with soot, walk round the tent with long poles or lances, singing in a mournful tone of voice, and striking the ground to frighten away demons; while others go and console the relatives. In other tribes, the body of the dead as well as that of his best horse is embalmed, smoked and dried, and carried to the forest, is covered only with branches. Among a few of these untutored children of nature, the corpse is buried as it is in civilized nations, but the best horse belonging to the dead is pinioned fast upon the grave mound, and left to his destiny. In every case, however, almost all the horses of the dead are immediately killed, that they may have the means of riding in the country of the dead; a few only being reserved to grace the last funeral pomp, and to carry the relics to their proper sepulchres. Some tribes bury their dead in large square pits about a fathom deep. The bones are put together, and each tied in its proper place; the skeleton is clothed in the best robe that can be got and adorned with beads and feathers, all of which they change once a year. They are placed in a row, sitting with the sword, lance, bow and arrows, *bolas*, and whatever else had belonged to the dead whilst living. These pits are covered over with trunks of trees, and canes or twigs woven together, upon which earth is thrown. These dreary habitations, kept with great care and opened once every year, are never far from the homes of the living. Around them are placed the bodies of their dead horses, raised upon their feet and supported by stakes. But the true Patagonians, after having dried the bones of their dead, carry them to a great distance from their habitations into the desert by the sea coast. When they are moved, they are packed up together in a hide, and placed upon one of the favourite horses of the deceased, kept alive for the purpose, and adorned with mantles, feathers, etc. The distance to which these bones are thus carried is sometimes six or seven hundred miles. The skeletons, when put together and adorned as above described, are set in order above ground, in a hut erected for that purpose, with the bones of their dead horses placed around them.

Their marriages are made by sale, the husband buying his wife of her nearest relations. Polygamy is allowed, but very few have more than one wife. The women are submissive and industrious; indeed their lives are but one continued scene of labour; they are forced to submit to every species of drudgery, and no excuse of sickness, will relieve them from the appointed labour; the husband is the lazy lord—the woman the oppressed slave.

Such was Patagonia in the year 1833, when the first attempt was make to Christianize that remote region. The Romish missionaries had preached Christianity to the Araucanians; but, although kindly treated by them, they had met with but little success in converting them from Paganism. Shut out by its remoteness and desolation from the visits of men, offering no advantage to the adventurer or reward to the industrious, Patagonia was left to continue in heathenish darkness, until in the year above mentioned a missionary spirit was awakened in her favour, and an effort was made to dispel the deep shadow which rested upon her. It had been stated that the Patagonians were a friendly race and of good capacity; and accordingly the North

American Board of Missions sent two pioneers to examine the capabilities of the country, and to try the possibility of establishing a mission there. These men, devoted and self-denying, spared no pains in the furtherance of their benevolent project; they remained nearly three months among the natives, and received most hospitable treatment from them, hungry barbarians as they were. But, although the disposition of the Patagonians towards them was good, they saw no likelihood of fruit to their labours; the provision, consisting only of horse flesh and ostrich eggs, was revolting to men brought up in the midst of civilization; even this could not always be obtained in sufficient quantity to satisfy the cravings of appetite; and altogether, so many dangers, anxieties, and discouragements were blended with their daily lives, that they became altogether disheartened. A vessel, cruising about among those remote and oozy islands of the South Pacific, touched on the shores of Patagonia, and, regretting to have accomplished so little and without any better prospect before them, the missionaries returned home, bearing with them an account of the impracticability of establishing a mission in that region of barrenness and starvation. Since that time, although efforts to spread Christianity in other parts of the world were made with zeal and vigour, Patagonia was left to herself; her heathen children were left to remain in ignorance and superstition, destitute of the means of grace, and without any man caring for their souls. No one for many years after this time could be found who was willing to take his life in his hand, to go and preach the kingdom of God to that benighted race.

CHAPTER II.

ALLEN F. GARDINER.

"Is he a heathen? Teach him thy better creed,
Christian! if thou deserv'st that name indeed."

"Give me the dauntless man,
Who flinches not from labour or fatigue,
But moves right on upon the path of duty."

ALTHOUGH Patagonia was discovered by Magellan in 1519, and was visited by Byron in 1764 and by Wallis in 1766, it seemed to possess but few attractions for adventurers. Little is known of it, extensive region as it is. No European nation has sought to colonize it, and it has never been thoroughly explored by travellers. In 1782 the coasts were surveyed by the Spaniards, whose chief attention was, however, directed to the examination of the straits of Magellan; previous to that time it was uncertain whether there was not a navigable channel further north than these straits. In 1826–1830 Captain King, in examining the western coast of Patagonia and Fuegia, found it to be bordered by a range of islands; Terra del Fuego was found to be intersected by a navigable channel, which he called Beagle Channel.

The Spaniards, who had sent missionaries among the tribes inhabiting Arauco, &c., endeavoured to found a colony on the coast of the Magellanic strait; not, however, with a view of benefitting or converting the natives, but as a resting place for their ships on their voyages from Chili to Peru. But in this bleak, mountainous, and barren region, with a rigorous climate, the inhabitants of a brighter land, born under sunny skies and nurtured on the food of civilized men, could not live; the whole colony perished from hunger, and the spot on which the settlement was made, is to this day called Port Famine. Similar attempts were made by the British to plant a colony at Port Egmont in the Falkland islands; but, with an inhospitable climate and a soil consisting of mountains and bogs, the effort has not prospered, further than to render it a watering place for ships bound to the Pacific.

So, for a long time, this Antarctic region was left uncared for. Ethiopia was stretching forth her hands to God, and the isles of the south, receiving gladly the news of salvation, but no one ventured into this land of darkness, to spread the light of truth among its benighted children. But the love of God, which never slumbers nor sleeps, awakened an interest in the heart of one, who, possessing a true missionary spirit, suffered no hindrance or prospect of hardship to deter him in carrying the message of peace to Patagonia, although it was warmly represented to him that his life would be the price of the venture.

Allen F. Gardiner was the name of this faithful servant of God. He was born at Basildon, in Berkshire, England, and was the fifth son of eminently pious parents. From infancy he showed a restless activity of disposition, love of adventure, and a strong taste for a nautical life. Upon one occasion when his mother went, as usual, into her children's nursery, she was surprised to find Allen asleep on the floor. On being aroused, he explained his not being in bed, by declaring that he intended, when he became a man, to travel all over the world, and therefore he wished to accustom himself to hardships.

It was not apparent, before he left home, that the decided piety of his parents had made any impression upon their bold and reckless boy; but the good seed had been sown; there was an influence deep and permanent, as it was silent and unperceived, which remained in him through the wildest seasons of his early life. He went to sea in 1810, and amidst all the ungodliness of his outward course, we find him ascribing his preservation, under circumstances of great danger, to his mother's prayers.

He was sent with a watering party to the river Yumbel in Peru; the boat upset, and the whole crew were with difficulty rescued from drowning.

The following day another party was sent on the same errand, a similar accident took place, and the midshipman in command was drowned. An impression was made on Allen's mind at the time by this incident, as well as by others of a similar nature; but it was only a fleeting one. He became an infidel and a scoffer in profession, and as daring in sin as he afterwards was fearless in duty. Yet with that strange inconsistency which often characterizes the ungodly, he showed himself weaker than a child in facing the ridicule of man. He gives a singular description of his own feelings, when some fit of remorse or remembrance of his home induced him once to go and purchase a Bible. When he came to the bookseller's shop he was ashamed to go in and ask for what he wanted. He paced up and down the street, waiting till there was no other customer within, for fear he should be seen; and when the quiet opportunity at last occurred, he thought how strange it must appear to the bookseller that he should ask for a Bible.

About the time when he was so near losing his life by drowning, he lost his mother, whose quiet influence had held him in check, as he entered the wild and daring life of a naval officer. The midshipman who was drowned was his friend; at such a moment of sorrow for one he loved, and gratitude for his own narrow escape, how would the thoughts unbidden fly homeward and imagine the mother at prayer for her young son! But now the thread was snapped which, like an electric wire, used, at a touch from home, to convey an instantaneous flash of home thoughts, home feelings, home affections, and home influence. There is a secret history in every heart which tells of this unseen power. Parents, brothers, and sisters—their kind and holy influence may be checked and resisted by distance, excitement, habits, companions—yet nothing but death can sever the invisible chain which connects the thoughtlessness of early manhood with some quiet but never-forgotten home.

And now one link was gone, and that one the tenderest. His mother and religion were inseparably connected in the mind of the young man; now the mother was dead, it seemed as if religion would die too. In the roving, reckless life of a sailor, he saw little profession or practice of true religion; what wonder, then, that in the midst of such excitement, even the form of religion was lost, and he periled his soul, like many thousands of young men, amid the headstrong passions of youth, the love of pleasure, and the eager pursuit of his professional occupations, to which he was devoted with all the ardour of his zealous nature!

No exact date can be assigned to his recovery from this dangerous state. Every one is subject, at intervals, to those inward admonitions by which God warns us of our sins and calls on us to flee from the wrath to come; and the fire, kindled early in the heart of Allen Gardiner by his home education, and which seemed to be dying out, would occasionally flash forth in gleams of transient brightness at seasons of death and danger such as we have described.

The year 1820 found him somewhat aroused to reflection, so far as to think over the past days of childhood, and the habits of prayer thrown away, and the words of Scripture forgotten, and he determined once more to read the inspired volume. But so long a time had elapsed since he had looked into the Scriptures that he now had not a copy, and deterred, by false shame, from purchasing one, he still "halted between two opinions."

During this year he served as lieutenant in the *Dauntless* which weighed anchor on the 30th May for Penang, by the way of Madras, and thence to China. Madras was reached; all who had never been there before were eager to land in order to experience the wonders of the Madras surf. Officers and crew were delighted, but there was little time for enjoyment, for in two days the ship was once more under weigh. They arrived at Penang in ten days, and had one week for rambling in the thick groves, observing the flowering shrubs, and admiring a luxuriance so great, that a single majestic tree towered above its fellows, carrying its lowest branches at the distance of 111 feet from the ground, and ascending to a height proportioned to the girth of its trunk, which measured upwards of twenty-eight feet.

It was while he was at Penang that the dawn of spiritual life was first perceived. Two letters arrived, one from his father, now unfortunately lost; the other from a lady who had known him from childhood, and felt a deep interest in him for his mother's sake. These letters Allen Gardiner acknowledged to have been instrumental, under God's blessing, in working a change in his character. This lady had been deeply pained at observing how far he was at that time from fulfilling his mother's hopes and wishes; and knowing that one of his sociable disposition and quick temper might probably run into great temptations, she spoke to him very earnestly before he left England, and gave him a short narrative of his mother's last days, which had been written by his father. This affectionate memento of his lost mother was the companion of his voyage, and often reminded him that he was the child of many prayers.

We give a few extracts from the lady's letter. After apologizing for the freedom with which she writes, she says: "Need I tell you, my dear Allen, that we are all by nature sinners,—lost, undone, guilty creatures; born into a world of sin and misery, and of ourselves utterly incapable of breaking the bonds of Satan, or of procuring the favour of the God we have offended? Need I tell you that if we remain in this state of sin, we must perish everlastingly, and that upon us will come the curse of eternal death—the death of the soul as well as of the body, the everlasting separation from God, and the everlasting society of Satan and evil angels? I am sure that you know these things, and that you also know there is a remedy. The seed of the woman, the Divine Saviour, is again and again promised to Abraham, as the seed in whom all the nations should be blessed. And in the fulness of time he came, taking upon him our nature that he might fulfil the law, that he might atone for the sins of the people, and set them an example that they should follow his steps. Christ's people are 'made willing in the day of his power,' and if we believe in him, we shall be tranformed into his image, translated out of the kingdom of Satan into the kingdom of God's dear Son.

"Nothing that is unholy or impure can enter heaven. The change spoken of in John iii. 3, must take place while we live (through the working of the Holy Spirit in our hearts), for as we are found in death, so shall we ever be; there is no repentance in the grave, nor pardon offered to the dead. . . . Unless we have a new heart, a heart of flesh, we cannot believe effectually."

There was much more in this letter of Christian admonition and scriptural argument, but we must not tire our readers by making further extracts. Allen Gardiner connected this letter with the prayers of his mother, and the earnest exhortations of his father. And when the ship pursued her voyage, the impressions made by them were not effaced.

Touching at Manilla they had an opportunity of visiting the celebrated tobacco manufactory. Gardiner says, "Here we found three thousand women seated around low tables arranged in regular order, and employed, some in beating out the leaf, others in rolling, cutting, and at length packing up cigars, 51,000 of which are usually made each day. The process is very simple. Each table is supplied with two cocoa nut shells, filled with a paste made of Indian corn, into which their fingers are occasionally dipped. With this substance the flattened leaf is smeared over, and when sufficiently moistened, rolled up with the palm of the hands and cut to the size required. Adjoining is a similar building, on the ground floor of which is a bullock-mill, for preparing snuff." He further adds; "The greater part of these people were Indians, and all professed Christianity. It is astonishing how popular the Romish religion has always become among Pagans, and how easily it is grafted upon heathenism, to which it is in many respects too much allied. It is but to lay aside one set of rude and unmeaning images, and to adopt others of a more attractive form—to barter stocks for saints, and turn devotion into a pleasing drama, and the Indian is conscious of no other difference."

After leaving Singapore, ten days brought them to Macao; but our limits will not allow us to accompany the officers in their rambles on permitted territory, nor in their trip to Canton, where they were amused by the determined and noisy method by which the Chinese beggars enforce payment for their departure; where they visited the temples and the sacred pigs, admired the contrivance and the ingenuity of the Chinese, and wondered why it was that these masters of ingenious mechanism should do all the work themselves, without aid from animals or machinery, there being only a triple division of labour—the buffalo for the plough, the horse for the mandarin, and the hands of man for everything else.

Some merchants at Macao had applied to the Admiral on the station to allow a ship to bring a cargo of specie from the Pacific. Gardiner's ship, the *Dauntless*, was the one appointed for the purpose, and therefore, six weeks after their arrival at Macao, they weighed anchor, and set forth on a trip which promised novelty to the elders, amusement to the juniors, and variety to all. Touching at Manilla, they were met by the news of the appalling ravages of the cholera, and they received a sad account of its destructive violence among the officers and crew of the *Leander*, the vessel from which Allen Gardiner had been exchanged into the *Dauntless*. On December 3rd they reached Penang, where this report was confirmed. The loss of many of his late shipmates had a powerful effect on the mind of Lieutenant Gardiner. In confirmation of this, the following extracts from two letters addressed by his father to his sister, are inserted.

"*April* 12, 1821.

"I have the high gratification of communicating to you that this morning I have a letter from dear Allen. It is dated at Macao, the 10th of October, and continued at Canton. He says nothing of his health; I therefore trust that he has been mercifully spared from the cholera, which prevailed on board the *Leander*. The voyage has proved delightful. The *Dauntless* touched at Penang, Malacca, Singapore, and Manilla, and at each place time was given to explore everything worth seeing. But that which affords me more satisfaction than I can express, is, that from various occurrences, and from a letter he received from me intended to have reached him at Spithead, but which only came to his hands at Penang, he has been led to review his past life, and his mind seems to have taken a religious turn. God grant that the impression may be lasting! When we meet, I will read to you the paragraph which has filled me with such joy. It must not, however, be mentioned, lest they may only be as the morning cloud and the early dew. Nevertheless, I do not think he would have written as he has done, ascribing to the grace of God the change that has taken place in his heart, unless his convictions had been of a very serious kind."

From another letter, dated April 14th, 1821, we may make one short extract, on the same subject: "May it please the Almighty Giver of all good to make these religious impressions lasting, and may he prove an example of every Christian temper, and every Christian grace, to all around him. Should not such an instance, as that before us, prove the inestimable advantage of a religious education? It has prevented many from sinking deep into the paths of the destroyer, and it has led others, who have fallen into gross sins, to reflect on their ways, and retrace their steps, having from early instruction a knowledge of the Scriptures, and the way of everlasting life."

In the mean time the *Dauntless* pursued her way to Trincomalee, where the business of refitting detained her two months, which time was spent by Gardiner in rambles through the islands. But a description of scenery, now so well known, of the rich cultivation and romantic defiles of the city of Kandy, surrounded by natural beauty, and yet blotted by the indelible stain of superstition, would be out of place here, so we will only mark the course of the *Dauntless*, which, after a voyage of two months and a half, arrived at Port Jackson. There they remained for five weeks, and leaving it on the 3d of August, passed the southern extremity of New Zealand and made the Island of Masafuero in six weeks, and still pursuing their voyage, they stood along the north shore of the Juan Fernandez, and on the 20th of September reached Valparaiso Bay. Here they came within the circle of news. The death of Napoleon and tidings of the war of Independence in South America were subjects of discussion; and as Callao, which was the point of destination for the *Dauntless*, was besieged by the English squadron, they remained at Valparaiso until they heard of the relief of Callao, for which port they sailed on the 27th of October. Whilst detained at Valparaiso, Gardiner, with two companions, set forth on a journey to visit Santiago and the Cordilleras, through a country which he afterwards travelled with very different feelings. Sailors are seldom good equestrians, and the long ride of ninety-nine miles tried their power of patience considerably. But they were resolved to see as much as possible in a short time, and, suffering no hardship to prove a hindrance, went forth boldly on their survey. Passing lightly by the picturesque appearance of the Chilian peasants with their high, conical hats and flowing ponchos, they ascended the heights in the neighbourhood of Santiago, took a mast-head view of the surrounding scenery, and wandered along the broad streets of the city in search of the cathedral, which, although incomplete, stands like a giant among the low roofed houses. They were greatly amused, on visiting the cloisters of St. Merced, to find a company of monks entertaining themselves with the very dignified game of hop-scotch. Bravely did their ecclesiastical feet hop from den to den, kicking the tile before them with all the elasticity of English schoolboys.

They were much surprized at the universal desolation of the city in the afternoon; the shops were closed, the streets deserted, business at an end, and all Santiago heavy in the enjoyment of after-dinner slumbers. Suddenly, at five o'clock, the whole city seemed to wake up with a start, and poured its inhabitants into the streets like a shower of hail. Visiting time was from five till eleven; and the hospitality always shown to strangers was speedily extended to Gardiner and his friends. In the course of the evening, other guests dropped in uninvited, according to custom, and music and dancing were the entertainment provided. During the intervals, preserves were handed round, and, according to the amusing etiquette of Santiago, it was customary to present the ladies with small portions on the end of a fork, each gentleman taking especial care to hold his pocket-handkerchief under the lady's chin, that no fragment might descend on her dress.

A striking contrast to this delicate manœuvre occurred a few days after, on an occasion which may be called a Chilian pic-nic. Starting forth one morning very early, in order to make the circuit of the city, they were sorry to find it cloudy. The distant mountains were entirely concealed; their summits, as the day advanced, appearing like so many islands floating above the mists that hung about their sides. Following the direction of the river, through lanes over-hung with the flowering branches of peach and plum trees, they reached the little valley of Nonoa, where they proposed to breakfast. Entering a small inn, prepared, as they believed, to take whatever was presented, they were amazed when a large bowl of olla-podrida made its appearance, without knife, spoon, or plate. While they looked at each other and the bowl, a little girl walked in, bringing some salt in the hollow of her hand, and carelessly threw it down on the table. But travellers must not be particular, and so, notwithstanding the prejudices of Englishmen in favour of cleanliness in general, and against dipping their fingers into dishes in particular, they managed, with some help from penknives, so that the meal was discussed.

On leaving Nonoa, they rode to the foot of the first ridge of the Cordilleras, where, after fording the Mapocho, a deep and rapid river, they reached a smelting house on the opposite bank, and saw various specimens of silver ore from the mines of San Francisco. From the elevated height of the spot where they stood, they had a magnificent view of this splendid country. The space was a rugged, broken, rocky height, covered with aloes and underwood; a cascade on one side, vineyards and orchards on the slopes of the hill, hamlets in the valley, and the city and plain of Santiago in the distance. The groups of *gauchos* or peasants were full of life, galloping across the plain. Every one seemed to ride; the women were all equestrians, and were to be seen mounted on a kind of chair-saddle on the right side of the horse.

With much reluctance they left Santiago for Valparaiso, from whence the *Dauntless* sailed on the 27th of October for Callao. The contrast between a voyage along the east and west coasts was very striking. Here the water was so smooth and the wind so uniform that the voyage might have been undertaken in an open boat. The clearness and serenity of a Chilian sky, and the lovely nights experienced on that coast, exchanged sometimes for the light veil of clouds which so often obscures the sun in those regions, were long remembered.

They reached Callao roads on the 22d of September, where they found a forest of merchantmen, chiefly English. On landing, everything seemed to point out the grand revolution which had just taken place. Soldiers were billeted everywhere, and many of the old Spanish residents were embarking for Spain.

Lima could not be seen to advantage at that time; but one feature of the place, although the fruit of war, gave our sailor friend much satisfaction. The Inquisition had been turned into the quarters of the conquering general, a sure sign of its complete suppression. Gardiner went over this den of tyranny and torture with deep interest; the ceiling of cedar was pointed out to him, but the exquisite carving seen in the great hall or place of judgment had little interest for him; he paid more attention to a figure of our Saviour, beneath which sat those judges who had decreed unrighteous doom to many, and was suggestive of that loving mercy which was not shown by them, and of that holy name which they so frightfully profaned.

Entering the public burying ground, Gardiner had some conversation with a priest, who gravely confessed that the poor were often interred without coffin or prayer. We can imagine the surprise expressed by Gardiner; but we cannot imagine the priest's reply, who appealed to his poverty, and said, that "unless masses were paid for, they could not be read."

The *Dauntless*, having taken on board its cargo of specie, sailed from Callao in November, on her return voyage to China. After an attempt to settle a dispute between the chief of one of the Marquesas and the proprietors of a whale boat which had been seized by the chief, Captain Gambier touched at Tahiti. This afforded our young friend an opportunity of witnessing the result of missionary effort, both there and in some of the neighbouring islands, in a manner which powerfully impressed a mind then really awakened to a sense of the value of souls. The observance of Sunday, by the natives was very striking. On the Saturday the Bay had been covered with canoes, and the decks of the English vessel were crowded with native visitors. On the Sabbath not one was to be seen, and the services on shore, which Gardiner and other of the officers attended, were observed by a most attentive and orderly congregation, numbering about two hundred and twenty.

On the next day, our friends went a few miles into the interior, to see a large church which the late king had erected. He had determined to build a house for the worship of God, which should surpass in size any that had been erected before for idolatrous purposes. The dimensions of this extraordinary building were 712 feet by 56. At its opening, in 1819, three pulpits were erected at equal distances, from each of which, at the same time, a sermon was delivered, the united audience amounting to six thousand people. Though this building was thus out of all proportion, we cannot but admire the motive which led to its erection. They also found six miles of good road already completed, a certain sign which showed civilization taking its proper place as an attendant of Christianity.

When the ship lay to off the Bay of Huahine, a large party went on shore. Gardiner remarks, "The surrounding scenery is extremely beautiful, coming up in every respect to the most romantic ideas I have ever formed of a South Sea island." And adds, "Although the mission to this island has not been established four years, everything indicated a more advanced state of society than was observable in Tahiti. To many of the houses paths were regularly made, neat wooden bridges were thrown across many of the streams that issued from the mountains, and several of the houses were weatherboarded and white-washed, in the European style. We heard that the usual Sunday congregation, including four hundred children who attend the school, is twelve hundred. In drawing a comparison between the state of improvement in this island and at Tahiti, it must be remembered that the ground was prepared by several of the chiefs and their people who had received instruction at Tahiti; so that idolatry was actually abolished before Christianity was established. As we bore away, a beautiful rainbow appeared over the island; a symbol, which, notwithstanding its general import to mankind, I could not but contemplate with peculiar reference to the happy valleys on which it seemed to rest, recalling to mind the promise, "All the ends of the world shall remember, and turn unto the Lord: and all the kindreds of the nations shall worship before thee."

Little more than three weeks after leaving Huahine, loss of health induced Gardiner to return home on sick leave, and a period of comparative quiet succeeded to the endless changes and excitements of his nautical profession. It was greatly blessed to him, as our sequel is about to show. A critical period of his life had now arrived, and he was about to make a great and decided step, one greatly important, both in time and for eternity.

CHAPTER III.

UNDER THE ROD.

He dreams how a veil drooping over the main
Shall be rent at the distant horizon in twain,
And how the New World, by the gospel's pure light,
Shall awake from the darkness of heathenish night.

THE temporary loss of health proved a great blessing to Lieutenant Gardiner. Opportunities of reviewing his past life were afforded him, and he was greatly humbled when he reflected on the ungrateful return he had made for special mercies granted to him. He knew that he was an object of special prayer to God, among very true friends. And now the wheel of life seemed to be stopped, in order that the wavering soul might be taught to pray; and he did pray. And while much time was given him to revolve what should be his future purpose, each day strengthened his determination to yield himself up fully to the service of God for the time to come.

The homeward journey became indeed a heavenward course; the young naval officer was being instructed by the Captain of his salvation. Soon after his return home, he offered himself to the London Missionary Society as a labourer in South America, the neglected state of the people in that beautiful region having deeply touched his heart. But the way was not opened to him at that time.

A journal which he kept while abroad, and a series of sacred meditations written at intervals, chiefly on Sundays, extending over a period of thirty years, will take the reader behind the scenes, and show the progress of a soul struggling with sin, enlightened, watchful, but conscious of much shortcoming, and grieving over a too frequent forgetfulness of a Saviour whom he wished to serve. We will give but few extracts from these papers, because there is a degree of impropriety in thus unveiling the soul's retirement, and only allowable when necessary to point out the actuating motives of a Christian, and the influence of God on his soul. Still, to show that inconsistencies of character are confessed and mourned over in private, and that the hand of God is recognized in all the providential affairs of life, may tend to quicken the negligent Christian, and rebuke the censorious, who are always ready to apply the charge of self-conceit and hypocrisy to those who deeply mourn in secret over every instance, which is given to the enemy to speak reproachfully.

After a prosperous voyage he arrived at Cape Town, in August, 1822. There everything reminded him of his former visit. On this occasion he wrote thus: "The last time I visited this colony I was walking in the broad way, and hastening by rapid strides to the brink of eternal ruin. Blessed be his name, who loved us and gave himself for us, a great change has been wrought in my heart, and I am now enabled to derive pleasure and satisfaction in hearing and reading the word of life, and attending the means of grace. I trust that this alteration has indeed been effected by the Spirit of God; yet I would not pause a moment to draw the contrast, except to give praise and gratitude to its merciful author, lest I should be drawn into the fatal snare of presumptuous self-confidence; but adoring my God for his goodness in not having consigned my soul long ago to the terrors of his indignation, I would carefully examine my heart as to the sincerity of its professions, and humbly implore at the throne of grace pardon for all that is past, and assistance to guide and strengthen me for the time to come."

And again at sea, "If Christians in the main are more culpable than Jews, how much must they have to answer for, who, like Timothy, have been taught the holy Scriptures from their childhood, and yet have despised their contents? Such are the aggravated sins which, if unpardoned, must weigh my guilty soul to the lowest hell. What return shall I make to the Lord for so early, so unmerited a display of his goodness? After years of ingratitude, unbelief, blasphemy, and rebellion, have I at last been melted? Alas! how slow, how reluctant have I been to admit the heavenly guest who stood knocking without! Nor had he ever been received, had not he himself prepared the way. And how is he now entertained? Ah! too unworthily. Too frequently am I ashamed to acknowledge the hand that was outstretched for my relief, to own the word that warned me from the brink of ruin, or to be seen supplicating that assistance, by which alone I can be prevented from stumbling over the dreadful abyss. Is this religion? Is this love to God? Is such my usual conduct when warned of any temporal danger?"

He arrived at home on October 31st, and a week afterwards he made his first proposal to be engaged in missionary work. The results, which he had seen with his own eyes in the Society Islands, disposed him to call the attention of the London Missionary Society to the still neglected heathen of South America; this memorial was accompanied with the offer of personal service; but the committee did not see their way clear to adopt his plans. About the same time also, he thought seriously of changing his profession, but, obstacles presenting themselves, he was led to decide against taking that step, and afterwards became firm in the conviction that St. Paul's rule is one for general observation, "Let every man wherein he is called, therein abide with God." This explanation will illustrate the following extract:

"I have this morning failed in an endeavour to obtain the privilege of being admitted to holy orders; but shall I dare to express myself disappointed? Had my will instead of God's been done, the very position might have become a snare. For some wise end it has been denied me. How dreadful would have been the breach of trust in an office of such awful responsibility! May this circumstance work for my good, by teaching me humility and resignation, and putting me more earnestly upon seeking the Lord in fervent prayer, in order to know and be enabled to perform his will, although it may be contrary to my own short-sighted views!"

The next seven years, in which he became a husband and a father, were spent in the privacy of domestic life. His wife, lovely alike in mind, person, and religious character, was a true help meet to him in the best things; and doubtless God used the drawing out of the home affections, from which his wandering life since early boyhood had excluded him, to develop the quick sympathies and deep attachments which afterwards resulted in loving devotion to the work entrusted to him.

In 1824 he was again called into active service, and in the capacity of first lieutenant to H. M. S. *Jupiter*, sailed for the coast of North America. On May 30th, 1825, he was transferred to H. M. B. *Clinker*, and remained in command of that vessel till she was ordered to England, eighteen months later, when he obtained his promotion as commander.

We will not intrude more than necessary into the privacy of family details; nor will we, having travelled with Gardiner abroad over sea and land, and accompanied him to England, enter his house uninvited, nor follow his every step like a shadow. Having given a view of the prevailing tone of his mind on the one great subject, we close his diary from 1825 to 1833, in which period he was not engaged in any public occupation, but in which we believe that God was fitting him for the work in which he was afterwards to be engaged.

In 1833, a succession of sore trials passed over him. Within twelve months he was called to part with an aunt, a dear child, and the beloved wife, whose delicate health had long been a cause of deep anxiety. He writes thus of his own feelings on this sad occasion :—

"My earthly comforts have been removed and I pass my days in sorrow. Blessed be God, he remembers that we are but dust. In my deep affliction, he has not left me without many and great sources of comfort. The chief of these is drawn from a review of the manifold grace and love which he vouchsafed to my dearest wife, making her last days the brightest and happiest of her life. Oh, what assurance of pardon, what joy and peace, and heavenly tranquillity, and ardent desire to be with her Saviour, did he infuse into her soul! He has prepared her for the enjoyment of his love, and is now filling her happy spirit with all the fulness of his grace and glory. Tasting, as I do, that the Lord is gracious, and feeling somewhat of his redeeming love to my soul, my spirit exults in her blessedness. It is only my earthly affections that weep and would call her back. Forty years have now passed over me—forty years of patience and long-suffering on the part of an offended God, and forty years of vanity on the part of his wayward and ungrateful child. Still a child I feel I am, and trust I ever shall be. The Lord has, indeed, of late graven upon me the marks of a child. He has chastised me sorely, and if I neither despise his chastisement nor faint under it, but pray that it may be sanctified to the saving of my soul, it will eventually result in blessings."

The "marks" of this time of chastisement were, indeed, impressed upon his whole future life, in the deeper tone of Christian thought and feeling it seemed to awaken. From this time his life was one of incessant action. He lived as a man who is looking at the things of time in the light of eternity. He had suffered keenly under the chastening hand of the Almighty, and was deeply sensible that the half-hearted way in which he had hitherto sought to serve God, not contented with making a general resolution to do better, he determined to consecrate his previous knowledge and all his energies to the service of Christ, according to a solemn act of self-surrender, which he had made by the bed-side of his dying wife.

The state of the heathen nations, still unreclaimed in different parts of the world, had made a deep impression on his compassionate nature; he had seen the wonderful results of missionary effort, under God's blessing, in the conversion of thousands of such poor outcasts, and he determined to seek out openings for the introduction of the gospel in any region where no attempt had yet been made.

The missionary is everywhere the grand pioneer of humanity, and in all ages and all countries Christianity and civilization have gone hand in hand. To become the pioneer of a Christian mission to the most abandoned heathens, was henceforward the grand aim of his life. Africa, that mysterious continent, which has so long been a little world of slavery, rapine, and blood; a home for pirates, the grave of enterprising travellers and noble-minded missionaries—Africa was the country to which his thoughts were first directed. It seemed to him as if a black thunder-cloud had settled on that unhappy country, leaving only two sparks of light on the south and west.

He looked at Cape Colony and saw it threatened by invasion from the Kafirs, but beyond Port Natal were the Zulu tribes and other populous nations, where a few daring English settlers were to be found, but where no missionary had ever penetrated. To these benighted regions, as yet unvisited by the messengers of the gospel, he resolved to go. After surmounting difficulties much of the same character as those experienced by Dr. Livingstone, arising alike from impassable roads, swollen torrents, wild beasts, and still wilder men, who, not actually hostile, would gladly have stripped the travellers of everything they possessed: with a few companions, he made his way to the fierce Dingarn, king of the Zulus; a savage, who was cunning as he was cruel, and had obtained the throne six years before, by bringing about the murder of his own brother and predecessor Charka.

He did not, however, enter on this new era of life without due preparation for the work he wished to accomplish, as the following extract will show. He writes thus on his last Sunday which he spent in the Isle of Wight.

August 24, 1834.

"This will, probably, be the last Sabbath which I shall spend in England for many months. Lord, enable me deeply to feel my unworthiness, humble me for my provocations, and give me such a sense of thy unspeakable goodness, that I may give myself wholly unto thee, as a living sacrifice in thy service. Lord, fit me for the work which thou hast inclined me to undertake. I feel my utter insufficiency, and would look only unto thee for strength and guidance."

On the 24th of August, 1834, he left England for the Cape of Good Hope.

Wellington, at sea, *Nov.* 11.

"We are now, by the good hand of our God upon us, within one day's sail of our destination; and as it is my earnest desire to take nothing in hand without seeking the aid and guidance of the Holy Spirit, I purpose to set this day solemnly apart for fasting and prayer, in the full expectation that the Lord will graciously attend to my cry, and make my path clear before me.

"O most holy and merciful Lord God, I beseech thee to prepare my heart now for solemn prayer, make me to feel abased in thy sight for all my sins and provocations against thee. No longer would I regard myself as my own, but bought with a price—and oh what a price! Lord, make me cheerfully to give up all, and follow thee. Thou, Lord, hast put it into my heart to devote myself to the service of the heathen. Oh that, if it be thy will, I may be a humble instrument in thy hand for good unto their souls! But I am as unequal as I am unworthy to do thee any service. I know, O Lord, that without thee I can do nothing that is pleasing in thy sight; but at the same time, I thankfully believe that with thee, all things are possible; as a little child, I would therefore come to thee. Lord, undertake for me, and prepare my way, incline the hearts of thy people to further my errand. Show me clearly the path of duty. Lord, if it be not thy will that I should go to the heathen, permit me not to deceive myself; but, if otherwise, oh, be thou my light, my way, and my refuge. Direct me, O Lord, what I should do, to whom I should apply, and where I should go. If it is not from thee, I desire not to go one step farther. And I would plead before thee thy gracious promise, 'Come unto me, all ye that are weary and heavy laden, and I will give you rest.' Lord, I am laden with pride and selfishness. This is the sin which (thou knowest) doth most easily beset me. It is my burden. Save me from its galling yoke, and bring me wholly to submit myself cheerfully to thy yoke, which is, indeed, easy, and thy ways are pleasantness. Having put my hand to the plough, may I never turn back! May thy strength be made perfect in my weakness."

On the 13th of November the *Wellington* anchored in Table Bay. He never did turn back.

CHAPTER IV.

THE MISSIONARY PIONEER.

"Is he a heathen? Teach him thy better creed,
Christian! if thou deserv'st that name indeed."

THE years 1834 and 1835 formed an important era in Captain Gardiner's life. From the year 1818, when the Keiskamma and the Great Fish rivers were ceded to Cape Colony, conciliating measures had been adopted towards the Kafirs, but without resulting in a substantial peace. The Kafirs were perpetually re-occupying parts of the ceded territory, carrying off cattle and provoking hostilities; therefore more rigorous measures were adopted, and the Kafirs were expelled from the ceded limits. A storm was brewing, silently but surely, and in 1834 it was known in the colony that war was inevitable.

Such was the position of affairs when Captain Gardiner entered the colony, with a determination of opening a way, if possible, for the introduction of the gospel among some of those warlike desperadoes, who had never yet been visited by the messengers of Him whose kingdom is peace.

He had heard much of an approaching war, but as it had not yet begun, he thought it would be possible to find his way through the various Kafir tribes, till he should reach the Zulus, to the North of Port Natal.

The Amakosa, Bechuana, Amaponda, the wandering Bushmen, and the Hottentots had received first, the Moravian missionaries, and afterwards, those of the Wesleyan, London, and French Protestant Societies. These, however, were scattered over a wide circle of country, but the far distant Zulus had as yet heard nothing of Christianity.

A few daring English settlers were even then to be found at Port Natal. It was time that some pioneer of missions should present himself where his countrymen were bold enough to remain. On the passage to the Cape, Captain Gardiner made the acquaintance of a Polish refugee of high rank, travelling under the assumed name of Berken; this gentleman entering into his spirit, accompanied him first to the missionary station, in Kafirland, and eventually to Port Natal itself.

At Graham's town, many tried to dissuade them from proceeding through a district so disturbed as that which now lay before them. But the more alarming the rumours of war, the more eager were our two friends to hasten their journey; and providing themselves with two wagons, thirty oxen, and an interpreter, they fearlessly traversed the ceded territory.

Two days after they crossed the frontier, the Kafir war broke out. "Poor Captain Gardiner!" was the remark of the friends at Graham's town; "we shall never see *him* again."

Having entered the Amakosa territory, they halted at Buffalo river, and whilst there, the natives drove the cattle off, and the man in charge, with difficulty, escaped with his clothes. A complaint being made to Tzatzoe, the chief, he readily agreed to send after them, and a well armed party proceeded to the hamlet where the suspected thieves resided. They could not, however, bring them to any kind of reason, and the travellers determined to refer the case once more to the chief; but in the mean time the cattle were driven back. The chief was now to be thanked and rewarded, and he who never lost anything for want of asking, thinking that wearing two shoes was carrying luxury too far, intimated that Mr. Berken could do nothing less than give him one of the two he wore.

At the next halting-place they were partially surrounded by a crowd of Kafirs, whose attitudes were by no means peaceful; and an order being given to yoke the oxen as speedily as possible, they endeavoured in the meantime to amuse the natives. They asked for a war dance; this occupied their attention, and served as a safety-valve, and gave vent to some of the vehemence of their impulsive natures. They yelled, and shouted, and declared that no white man should again enter their country, or eat the bread of their children; but ended in allowing our travellers to depart peaceably.

From this time forward, the strictest watch was necessary to prevent the loss of all that was portable. The restless Kafir prowled round his prey in the darkness of night; his noiseless feet disturbing no dream of the weary sleeper, but waking with the early dawn, he might see the dark form of his nocturnal visitor stealing quietly away. They now entered the district of the Amapondas, a mountainous country, but studded with missionary stations. The Amapondas were friendly to the English, and Faku, their chief, would gladly have joined them in a war with the Amakosa.

A delay at the Umzimvubu, led to an interview between Captain Gardiner and the chief. When the former rode up, he found Faku sitting in state under a roof of shields, trying a rain-maker for restraining the clouds, and thereby causing drought. The rain-maker defended himself. Faku, however, broke up the assembly, by coming forward and shaking hands with his visitor. On hearing his errand, he said, "The Zulus are an angry people, and will kill you. You had better not go to their country."

The travellers found their way further beset with difficulties. The distance which lay before them was much greater than they had been led to expect, and thus provisions fell short. Mr. Berken, becoming much fatigued, took charge of the wagons, but the dauntless and untiring Gardiner rode forward, impatient to begin the work on which his heart was so resolutely set. But the riders met with many hindrances, which more than made up for the increased speed of their movements. Unacquainted with the route, they were often misled by hippopotami paths, and had to retrace their way. The horses, on more than one occasion, sank suddenly into a morass or quicksand, and had to be extricated by mining with the hands, one leg being released at a time.

A whole night Captain Gardiner spent without food or shelter on a river side, with hippopotami snorting and mosquitos humming around.

This river was the Umkamas, and being high and rapid, a canoe was formed of ox-hide, and stretched on a frame-work of poles. In this, as no one but the Captain had any idea of the management of a boat, he made the first attempt to cross, with the only swimmer of the party. They landed without difficulty, but to return for their companions was found to be impossible, from the force of the current. The next morning, one of the horses having been made to swim over from the other side, Capt. Gardiner proceeded without delay to Port Natal, arrived there about sunset on the same day, and sent back supplies to the men at the Umkamas.

The whole journey is curiously illustrative of Capt. Gardiner's rapid and decided movements. In his haste to proceed, he had left Mr. Berken and his wagons at the Umzimvubu. Twice afterwards he left part of his advanced company behind, and arrived at Port Natal with a single attendant. He did not linger there. In two days he was again on the road, with a fresh wagon and team of oxen, but these were sent back from the Ungani, for though the river was practicable for men and horses, it was too high for a wagon to cross. At the Tugala, for a similar reason, he left his horses; the number of alligators which infest the river increasing the difficulty of the passage.

Thus, when they entered the Zulu territory, the whole cavalcade was reduced to three travellers on foot, Gardiner, Cyrus the interpreter, and Umpondombeni, a Zulu, who from this time became the Captain's faithful attendant. They reached the Tugala on Feb. 3d. But long before they arrived there, the distant hills of the Zulu country were seen. "I shall never forget," said Gardiner, "the interest with which I perceived the first curl of smoke rising from a distant village in that direction. I forgot all fatigue on finding myself on Zulu ground, and thanked my God for having thus far prospered my way." While Captain Gardiner, having crossed the Tugala, is making his way into the interior of an unknown country, it may be well to give a short account of the people he was now about to visit.

The authentic history of a tribe of Africans is not easy to obtain. Like the central wilds of their mysterious continent, they are lost in obscurity.

The petty chief rules his wretched serfs with iron hand, and crushes every symptom of rebellion with death. But let the bold and watchful chief be weakened by the advance of years or misfortune, the assassin's hand is ever ready at the bidding of some unscrupulous adventurer, who steps in and seizes the power he longed for. A native African will obey as long as the ruling despot has the power of enforcing his commands, and then he is willing to transfer his allegiance to the successor, no matter how he attained his elevation.

The successful warrior rules his tribe till a warrior, more successful than he, destroys him, and reigns in his stead. It signifies little to a tribe who may be its chief, provided the tribe maintains its ascendancy among the surrounding people. Three qualities are necessary to a successful chief. He must have daring enough to plot against his master; he must be careless of his own life, and still more so of the lives of others; and he must have mind enough to keep his warriors employed.

This was the character of Charka, the able but unprincipled king of the Zulus. He obtained his sovereignty by assassination. Reckless of danger to himself or others, he was continually at war, and his rule over his subjects was most arbitrary. His own territory extended from the sea to the Quathlamba mountains; these, however, formed no barrier, for his troops frequently passed them, depopulating whole villages, and driving the inhabitants in hordes upon the colony. Charka was extending his conquests southward, and alarming Faku, king of the Amapondas, when the blow of an assegai, ordered by his brother and successor Dingarn, terminated his life. When Captain Gardiner undertook this journey to the Zulu country, Dingarn had been king for six years. He had withdrawn his forces to the north of the river Tugala, but the few English settlers at Port Natal were kept in continual alarm on account of his threatened forays after deserters.

Lieutenant Farewell was the first settler in Natal, and his fate, as related to Gardiner, was sufficient to deter any one less brave to advance. He was passing through a tract of country occupied by a revolted tribe of Zulus, who had left their home and settled near the Umzimvubu, marking their course with devastation. They enticed Lieutenant Farewell some distance away from his people, on pretence of selling him some cattle, and treacherously murdered him together with his attendants.

Such were the wild people to whom Captain Gardiner was now intent on bringing the knowledge of the gospel, and it required no ordinary boldness to carry on such a scheme; but under the conviction that he ought to do all he could for the glory of the Saviour, who has promised his help to those whose aim is to obey, he crossed the Tugala, and advancing into the country of the Zulus, effected an interview with Dingarn.

It was difficult to make the chief understand the

object of this visit. What was God and God's word, and the nature of the instruction proposed, were subjects he could not comprehend. When the many advantages accruing to other nations from the reception of Christianity were represented to him, he seemed inclined to be favourable, and asked if his people could learn; but he evidently regarded the whole as an impossibility. He, however, gave a partial consent that a house should be built, and expressed a desire to see *the Book* of which Gardiner had spoken so much, and bade him bring it on his next visit.

Three days afterwards, a second intervew was had with this formidable chief, who immediately opened the conversation with the question, "Have you brought the Book?" A pocket Testament was produced. "Read," commanded Dingarn; and passages from the holy volume were read, pointing out the power and omniscience of God, the nature of sin, and the future day of judgment. "Who is God?" said Dingarn. "Whom will he judge? Will my people be at the judgment? Can I ever learn his word?" Yet, notwithstanding this seeming interest in the subject, he resorted to evasions whenever he was asked to accept of a permanent Christian teacher, referring him to his two principal Indunas. These dignitaries, affronted because he had not made his business known to them before he went to the king, tried every means in their power to insult him and thwart his plans. The people also followed the example of their superiors, and jeered him and his companions as they passed by. At length the behaviour of the Indunas changed. Gardiner was admitted to more frequent interviews with Dingarn, and he waited a whole month in hopes of receiving a distinct answer.

Captain Gardiner and his friends, in the mean time, received a frightful impression of the horrors of savage life, from what they saw of Dingarn's conduct, which rendered him more than ever desirous of establishing Christianity and rooting out heathenism. Some suspicion was thrown upon Gonjuana, Dingarn's brother, as having plotted against him. True or false, the suspicion was enough for the tyrant, who was a fratricide himself. The unhappy wretch was seized, with his servants; they were cruelly beaten with sticks on all parts of their bodies, "to take away their strength," as it was said; and then, driven to the place of execution, were dispatched with further blows on the head. Gonjuana, in consideration of his being a king's son, was strangled. The tragedy, however, was not yet ended. With a man of rank, among these people, live or die all his dependents, and Gonjuana was ruler over ten villages. His death was the signal for the destruction of his doomed subjects. Assembled by a message from the king, the inhabitants of the ten villages dependent on the murdered prince, were treacherously attacked and stabbed by those who had just been conversing with them, apparently on the most friendly terms; and few survived to tell the tale.

The only remedy for these sad cruelties that occurred to Captain Gardiner, was the preaching of the gospel. He had the strongest faith in the power of Christ to change the hearts even of men like these, and was, therefore, very anxious as to the success of his present attempt.

At the end of a month, no progress having been made, Captain Gardiner requested an audience with the king; Dingarn sent him to the Indunas. The Indunas were dancing and could not be disturbed. Next morning preparations were made for the removal of the whole population to a town distant about ten miles. No questions could be asked now; Captain Gardiner therefore accompanied the expedition. It consisted of about nine hundred men, and had a war-like aspect; they moved in single file, and were joined by the men from two towns on their way. Dingarn was proud of his troops, and fond of being received with noise and extravagant antics. He enquired of Gardiner if his king visited his people; and how he was welcomed when he made his appearance. Gardiner immediately tossed up his hat into the air, and gave three cheers, which seemed to give great satisfaction.

As soon as the march was over, a series of public dances were to be-celebrated, and Gardiner felt that much time was passing away, without any hope of establishing his mission. A pocket Testament and spoon formed his whole baggage; the floor of a hut was his bed, and a saddle was his pillow.

The long wished-for interview was at last granted. The little Testament was produced, but the two Indunas expressed themselves with great decision; "We do not want to learn it. If you will instruct us in the use of the musket, you may stay;" and Dingarn closed the subject by saying, "I will not overrule the decision of my Indunas."

Keenly as he felt the failure, in the hour of disappointment he wrote that, by these means, "God not only proves and prepares the instruments by which he designs to work, but shows us that his purposes will ripen and unfold without their aid."

There was now no use in remaining longer; and retracing his way to the Tugala, he had the pleasure of meeting Mr. Berken, and the friends went back together to Natal. Here they found many Zulu refugees from Dingarn's cruelty; and therefore, full of missionary enterprise as ever, and in no wise daunted by his late failure, Gardiner established Sabbath services, and schools for their children.

Immediately on their arrival, they received a letter signed by eight residents of Port Natal, expressing their great regret for the unfavourable reception given by Dingarn, but also declaring their approbation of a missionary establishment at Natal, and promising to support and aid in the promotion of industry and religion, by every means within their power. Mr. Berken gave his friend every possible aid in his plans of usefulness; and determined on making this place his future residence, sailed for the colony, for the purpose of purchasing stock and supplies for the farming establishment he was now commencing. He sailed in the *Circe*, which vessel never reached her destined port.

Upon a threatened invasion of the Zulus, Gardiner made a second attempt to conciliate their savage chieftain. The population of Natal consisted of about thirty English, a few Hottentots and hunters, and three thousand Zulu refugees; the number of the last being greatly increased by the addition of runaways from the territories of Dingarn. These he threatened to reclaim with an armed force, and as the people of Natal knew he was one likely to put those threats into execution, they were kept in a state of perpetual alarm.

Gardiner was successful in gaining him over to enter a treaty on the following terms. A promise on his part to leave the present inhabitants of Natal unmolested, and a refusal on their part to admit any more deserters from his territory.

This treaty has been subjected to much severe reprehension. But the colony, including some thousand refugees from Dingarn's territory, was entirely at his mercy, and therefore a treaty which should secure the lives of all those resident there, at the expense of refusing to receive any future deserters, might be deemed not more politic than necessary.

Some address, however, on the part of Gardiner, who was the bearer of the treaty, had to be used to conciliate this formidable chief. He travelled on horseback, accompanied by his interpreter, two Zulu servants, and a wagon; and in six days arrived at the head quarters of Dingarn. The ceremony of offering presents was highly agreeable to his savage majesty. A pair of naval epaulettes, which were forthwith sewn on his red cloak, some coloured prints of English scenes, which gave occasion to many questions, and a telescope, the first he had seen, gave him no little pleasure, and put him in a most conciliatory mood.

At last came the decisive interview. Dingarn gave his "fast word," but said that the whites would be the first to break the treaty,—a prediction unhappily fulfilled, despite of Gardiner's effort to hold them to their word.

A conversation relative to the mission and the Holy Book followed, and the Indunas, overjoyed at the treaty, offered no opposition.

But further proceedings were stopped by the continued desertion of the Zulus, and Gardiner, feeling that his pledged word must be sacredly kept, returned to Natal, to see that the terms of the treaty were fulfilled. He knew that no other course would give security to the white settlers or refugee Zulus, and therefore insisted that the deserters, now on their way, should be sent back. Four runaways, (the only persons ever sent back,) were, according to the treaty, given up. Captain Gardiner accompanied them, in order that he might, if possible, obtain their pardon from Dingarn, and teach them what Christ had done for sinners.

At Congella, Dingarn received them, and appeared in so good a humour that Captain Gardiner was able to plead for their pardon. This was denied, but a promise was obtained that their lives should be spared, which however was not kept, for no sooner had Gardiner gone, than they were put to death. That Dingarn was somewhat afraid of his late visitor, seems evident from this act of duplicity. He subsequently published an order that no trade should be allowed with Port Natal, and that none but Gardiner should be permitted to enter his country.

He returned then a third time to the king, to explain that he had had no power to prevent the breach of promise, for Dingarn was at that time greatly incensed at the unfair dealings of two Natal traders, who had enticed deserters, at the very time of the agreement to receive no more. Nevertheless, he at once expressed his readiness to treat with *him*, and the Natal settlers through him, but holding him answerable for any breach of agreement on their part. Gardiner represented that he had no power whatever. "You must have power," was Dingarn's reply. "I give you a large tract of country; you must be the chief over all the people there." This unexpected proposition made a journey to Graham's Town necessary, in order to consult Sir Benjamin D'Urban on the propriety of its acceptance or refusal.

The journey to Umzimvubu, and through the country of the Amapondas, was by no means dangerous. Faku, their chief, had from twelve to fifteen thousand men at his disposal, and was on friendly terms with the English. But as they approached the country of the Amakosa, who were then at war with the colony, the travel became more hazardous. Gardiner's original plan was to ride in the night, with the swiftest horses he could procure. But no guides would undertake the journey; he therefore retraced his steps to Bunting. The locusts on some parts of the road were so numerous that the ground could scarcely be seen, and numbers were crushed under the horses' feet. The travellers were in great want of food on their arrival at Bunting at sunset, not having tasted anything since an early breakfast on the previous day.

Passing by Faku's Amapondas, from whom no assistance could be obtained, Gardiner once more crossed the Umzimvubu, and found himself among the Amahoash, whose chief, Tpai, was a thorough specimen of an African despot. He was very ready with questions as to the part Dingarn was likely to take in the Kafir war, and on the movements of the English army, but when asked for guides his replies were unsatisfactory. Not an individual would volunteer, therefore it was necessary to go back to Port Natal.

Great was the anxiety caused by this detention. Nature was beautiful in this wild spot, but in the nightly bivouac who could contentedly admire her vagaries, with a mind vexed and tormented with disappointments and delays?

Another route was now to be attempted. For this the equipments consisted of two wagons, fifty-one draught oxen, twelve calves for food; allowing two span of twelve oxen for each wagon. Though the country was much broken, they made tolerable progress for four days, when one of the wagons became fairly imbedded in a swamp, and had to be dug out.

The comforts and luxuries of civilized life are so numerous and appear so necessary, that however familiar one may be with African wanderings and traveller's tales of life in the bush, it is really hard to realize the long drawling journey of a South African traveller, or the tedious, vexatious delays which he must endure.

The wagon being dug out of a swamp, a hill rises straight in the path. One wagon must be slowly dragged up by both teams of the grunting oxen, which must go back and fetch the other. Then comes the crossing a river; the shouting, screaming tones of the drivers; the snorting, grunting, half-rebellious voices of the annoyed beasts, the crushing of the wood beneath the ponderous wheels, are altogether exciting. And then the dash into the water, the floundering of the oxen, the exertion to keep the baggage dry, add no little to the previous bustle. But when the road is unknown, the guides ignorant, the passage of the mountains extremely doubtful, a better lesson in patience under difficulties, than such a journey as was this, it is not easy to conceive.

Guides were obtained by Captain Gardiner, but they deserted when it rained; fortunately the rain was not of long continuance, and the so-called guides returned, but as the track was lost after a few days' journey, they confessed their ignorance of the way, and were therefore dismissed.

Gardiner now attempted to steer his way by the points of the compass, but at the evening bivouac, it was too often found that little progress had been made in the right direction.

Once as he was pushing on ahead of his wagons, in search of a practicable pass, he ascended from crag to crag, leading his horse, he was overtaken by a thunderstorm, and a thick mist rising, nearly concealed the path. He unsaddled his horse, and seating himself on a rock, prepared to pass the night where he was. Undaunted by this new difficulty, patient as ever, and without the remotest hope of assistance from his party, he "had recourse to that sure refuge, a throne of grace," and He who is the hearer of prayer, listened to his cry and delivered him. Through an opening in the mist, he was soon enabled to perceive the route by which he could retrace his steps; and, although it soon after became as thick as ever, he was able to proceed, and after a tedious walk by night-fall, succeeded in rejoining the party with the wagons.

Wherever he might be, it was Gardiner's practice to have public service with his companions on Sunday, and if Kafirs were with him, a second service in the Kafir language. And now here, among the Quathlamba mountains, where probably divine service had never been held before, the sound of praise and prayer ascended to heaven. Where could be a more appropriate temple for worship of the Most High than in this mountain scene of great magnificence, exhibiting as it did many of the sublimest characteristics of the Alps—rocks rent, and scattered about in shapeless fragments, in others standing upright, like the ruins of ancient castles. No passage could be found among these craggy obstacles, and after an unsuccessful attempt to cross the chain, it was determined to follow the course of the mountains, which run parallel with the coast, until they should reach the colony near Stormberg. Often after a travel of ten miles a day, they found they had advanced only two or three from the last bivouac.

On crossing the Umzimkulu, the foot-marks of men and a dog were seen; this proved that the country was inhabited or visited by man, and, a few days after, a well-beaten path was traced to the brink of a cave. Here they found marks of fire, remnants of mats, bunches of Indian corn, bowls, and head-plumes; but the print of horses' feet showed plainly that a party of Amakosa had retreated to this mountain fastness. The cave was capable of containing one hundred persons; the Kafirs could not have left it more than six or seven weeks. A life in the bush sharpens the conjectural faculties, and the desertion of this strong-hold seemed to be the notification of peace with the colony. Full of this hope and that, consequently, the usual road to the colony was open, Gardiner now thought only of reaching the coast by the nearest route. After a fortnight's difficult travelling this was effected by eight of the party, with three pack oxen; the rest were left to follow at leisure: Large herds of gnu frequently rushed past the strange intruders, their necks covered with shaggy hair, and their white tails floating in the wind. Whole colonies of baboons were sometimes disturbed, some of them nearly the size of a man; and while the larger specimens sat and grinned at the travellers from the rocks and trees, the females carried off their young in great alarm.

When they arrived at Bunting, they were most kindly received, and while they tarried there waiting for the wagons, two Wesleyan missionaries, direct from the colony, gave the joyful announcement that all hostilities had long since ceased, and a treaty had been entered into with Kheeli the Kafir chief.

All difficulty was now removed, and Captain Gardiner accompanied the missionaries back to the colony. They travelled on horseback to Graham's Town. The traces of war were, in many places, quite evident; the mission houses were burned, but the missionaries were at their posts.

Near Butterworth they visited Kheeli, in hope of obtaining horses. They were told that the English had taken all their horses. They succeeded, however, in obtaining guides to the Kei river, to which point they accompanied them, but could not be induced to cross. "On gaining the British side," says Gardiner, "we knelt down and offered up a prayer of thanksgiving to the God of all our mercies, by whose good providence we had been so mercifully protected on our journey." On reaching Fort Warden, Gardiner was supplied with fresh horses to King William's Town, the head quarters, where he was received with great interest and provided with a military escort to Graham's Town.

He found, on his arrival there, that Sir Benjamin D'Urban was at Port Elizabeth, one hundred miles distant. By riding through part of the night, our missionary pioneer accomplished the distance in twenty-six hours; had a most satisfactory interview with the Governor, who gave his consent that Gardiner should accept of Dingarn's offer, and sent a letter expressive of his satisfaction of the measure, by a vessel then about to sail for Port Natal.

Thus encouraged, our unwearied pioneer sailed at once for England, in the hope of inducing the Church Missionary Society to make use of the opening thus provided.

CHAPTER V.

HAMBANATI AND THE ZULU MISSION.

"Methinks these beauteous spots remain,
Like virtues in the savage breast,
Mementoes that we still retain—
Of purity, at first impressed,
Brief notices of Eden's joy,
That Sin itself could not destroy.—GARDINER.

THE first object of Captain Gardiner on reaching England, was to present a despatch from Sir B. D'Urban to the Home Government, urging upon them the importance of colonizing Port Natal; and at the same time offered for their disposal the extensive grant of land he had himself received from Dingarn. The Governor's proposal was negatived at that time, although it has since been found necessary to act in accordance with the suggestions then made. A letter was addressed to the committee of the Church Missionary Society, detailing the recent researches among the Zulus, and earnestly imploring them to avail themselves of the opening now made.

The Society did not at once consent, for want of

men, but on the 3d of May, at the annual meeting in Exeter Hall, an appeal was made in behalf of a mission to the Zulus, not only in a formal resolution, but with all the enthusiasm of Gardiner himself. The success of these appeals may be seen at once from the fact that, on the 9th of November, instructions were given to the Rev. Francis Owen, his wife and sister, on occasion of their departure for the Cape of Good Hope, to commence the mission to the Zulus. These excellent persons, who had volunteered for this special mission, were urged to be active and laborious in acquiring the native language, in translating parts of the Scriptures, and in forming a Christian school for Zulu children.

During Captain Gardiner's stay in England he married again; and accompanied by his wife and three children, embarked together with the Owen family, for the Cape of Good Hope.

They landed at Cape Town on March 2d, 1837, and were kindly received by the Governor, who consented to preside at a meeting for the formation of a Church Missionary Association at Cape Town.

Thus far all was promising. Captain Gardiner had reached the country which he hoped to make the land of his adoption. Missionaries were on their way to the Zulus, and he was about to follow. But "whom the Lord loveth he chasteneth, and scourgeth every son whom he receiveth." The destroying angel was once more commissioned to enter the family. His eldest child, a blooming lively girl of twelve years of age, was the victim, and without showing any definite symptom of disease, she gradually faded away. The sea voyage, it was hoped, would restore her to health. Then the wagon journey through the colony would certainly benefit her. But no; neither availed. Although she entered into the varying adventures of such a journey with liveliness and spirit, it was but too apparent when they arrived at Graham's Town that she was nearing her everlasting rest. But as her father watched her gradual decline, his heart was not all sorrow; he had the comfort of witnessing a marked growth in grace; and of knowing that in view of her expected change, "all was well." She fed upon the 51st Psalm, and the Gospel of St. John, and rested her soul in simple confidence on the Saviour's words, "Him that cometh unto me I will in no wise cast out." She died on the voyage from Port Natal to Port Elizabeth, May 11, 1837, and was buried at Berea. It seemed a dark providence. The thoughts of Allen Gardiner had joyfully centred for a long time on the spot which he now reached in sorrow; and his first act on landing was to provide a grave for his firstborn. There the mourning family laid down the lifeless flower. They looked above for comfort, and they found it. Blessed is the assurance that tells us, "What ye know not now, ye shall know hereafter."

Gardiner had, however, little time to brood over his sorrow, for other cares claimed his attention.

As soon as the fact of his arrival was made known, and it was learned that he was about to settle in the Zulu territory, the people crowded around their English chief, to express their willingness to live under his authority; and soon their huts, springing up about his home, near the river Umtongata, about half-way between Port Natal and the Tugala, formed the beautiful village of Hambanati, or "Come with us."

As soon as he had settled his family in temporary houses, Gardiner felt it important to make a visit to Dingarn. In the course of his journey he halted at a Zulu village, and the Incosi-case, or chief woman, was informed that this was God's day, and was asked if she were willing to attend the services, or if any of her people wished to do so. Her reply was by no means peculiar to her,—the same is often heard in Christian towns,—"She could not go herself, and did not think any of her people would," a prediction which proved most true. Services were however held, prayers were offered up, one of the Zulu baggage-bearers was instructed, and an All-seeing eye above witnessed the love which his servants bore to Christ.

A journey of four days brought Gardiner into Dingarn's presence. He found him seated on a rock, following with his glass every party which approached from the direction in which he expected his presents. The presentation of those sent by the colonial government was made in due form. A pair of epaulettes, several yards of red cloth, some military buttons, a package of pink tape, and a silver watch, with gilt chain and seals.

Dingarn was greatly pleased with all the things, and was as much enraptured as a child by the exploit of winding up the watch. A pair of worsted slippers were soon fitted on his great feet, upon which he observed to the wondering spectators, "He took my measure before he went."

At length the presents were all discussed, and the chief was ready to listen. He was informed that the teachers for whom Gardiner had gone to his own country, were now on their way; and when asked where they were to build, he replied, at Unkunginglove. This was the place which Gardiner had selected, and he expressed his satisfaction and thanks accordingly.

Dingarn however replied that he wished Gardiner to build also at Unkunginglove, but when he was made to understand that operations were commenced at Hambanati, from whence visits could be easily made, he made no objection.

Allusion was next made to the grant of territory, as a ground for the present request, that a portion of the country might be secured to Gardiner. At first the crafty chieftain appeared disposed to forget that he had promised anything, but at length gave his consent on condition that the terms of treaty should be faithfully kept. This Gardiner promised should be done in strict justice, but on proposing that a document, fixing a definite boundary, should be drawn up, to which Dingarn should affix his mark, the chief deferred this transaction until his Indunas should return. He dictated a letter in the meantime to the King of England, giving to him, but in a very indefinite manner, the territory occupied by Faku, the chief of the Amapondas, of whom he was evidently jealous, as he was known to be favourable to the English. The same feeling extended to the people of Port Natal, and therefore Dingarn did not disguise his intention of advancing his people nearer to the object of his jealousy, and for this purpose to occupy part of the territory granted to Captain Gardiner. The position of the latter was one requiring great circumspection; but glad that Dingarn had consented to his settling on the Umtongata, he took up his residence there.

As he returned, he visited two American missionaries; these were only permitted to enter the territory in consequence of the agreement between Captain Gardiner and Dingarn. Sunday was spent at their station, when Mr. Champion addressed about ninety natives in their own language.

The buildings at Hambanati proceeded; and an attempt was made to pay the natives for their work on the system of barter. They were to receive blankets, kilts, etc., for so many days' work. But murmurs of dissatisfaction, by no means pleasant to hear, arose; not on account of the work, but to the establishment of a system of payment. They were ready to work when required; all they wanted for it was an occasional present from their chief. "For what," said they, "would the Zulus think when they heard they had been buying from their chief?"

On a second visit of Captain Gardiner to Dingarn, Mr. Owen accompanied him. They found the chief at Unkunginglove; presents were made, and fireworks exhibited, which excited great interest and promoted good humour.

Mr. Owen, who had heard much of the savage cruelty of Dingarn, could not realize the character given of him, in the individual before him. "There was nothing sanguinary in his appearance," he says, "and I could hardly believe that those hands had been so often imbrued in blood."

On Sunday, when Mr. Owen sent to request permission of Dingarn to preach to the people, he desired him to come to the Issigordlo, or king's house. There, then, was the gospel of Jesus Christ preached in the presence of a fierce Zulu chief. Dingarn listened with great attention, and an incredulous smile occasionally showed that he comprehended what he heard. He asked many questions. Mr. Owen spoke of the resurrection of the Saviour, and the future resurrection of mankind. "Why do they not get up now?" he inquired. Mr. Owen's apt reply was, "Because God hath appointed the day. But now he hath commanded all men, everywhere, to repent." "How can they get up again?" "Will they have the same body?" "Will they see each other?" "Will they know their friends?" "Will it be Sunday when they get up?" "When will the last day come?" etc. These questions having been answered chiefly in Scriptural language, the missionaries retired to their hut, and in the afternoon held a service for their own company.

Their presence on the next day was required by Dingarn. After an examination of the fireworks and presents of Mr. Owen, the chief consented that a hut similar to the one built for him at Unkunginglove should be built at Congella. Although an address was desired in presence of the assembled people, and in the same words used on the previous day, little attention was paid. As in civilized countries, a smart bonnet or a shabby coat often attracts the attention from prayers or the sermon, so in the Zulu country, a poor blind man, who was present, excited the ridicule and attracted the observation of the whole audience. Captain Gardiner says, "According to the eye of sense it was a most discouraging commencement, but He, who can make the weak things of the earth to confound the strong, can and will in his own time manifest his love and truth to those who are now sitting in darkness and the shadow of death."

Dingarn had erected a hut for Mr. Owen on a hill two miles from the town. On their return journey they chose a site for another mission hut at Congella. Near the Tugala, an immense flight of locusts, coming from the north, appeared at first like a mist, partially covering the mountain tops, but in a very short time the whole atmosphere was, as it were, charged with them, some settling, others rapidly passing in myriads overhead. In a few seconds the trees were so covered with them that they appeared as if divested of all their leaves, the beautiful green of the mimosa being changed to a deep russet brown. They appeared to be merely resting for a time, as on examination of some of the trees on which they had remained the longest, it was found that the leaves had not been eaten.

Another journey had now to be made to the Zulu chief, in consequence of a message from him, that his army was returned, and he wished Gardiner to come and see it.

We must pass over the particular detail of this review, but as the whole led to an affair of political importance we mention a leading incident. The Zulus on entering the country of their enemy, Moselekatse, captured a few prisoners whom they took for guides. After a severe skirmish with a small body of men posted among some rocks, they advanced till they encountered the main body of their foes, and gained a decisive victory over them, as was evident from the amount of cattle brought home, numbering six thousand head, two thousand having died or strayed by the way. But the conquest cost them the lives of one thousand men.

They had found a pistol, which gave the Induna Umthlella an opportunity of professing a great contempt for fire-arms. "What are guns for?" said he; "we need not be afraid of them—guns are nothing—they only make a noise and do no harm." This was their boastful story; but an inspection of the captured cattle gave some uneasiness to Captain Gardiner, for the usual mark of the Dutch Boers was visible on many of the animals. They might have taken them from Moselekatse's people, but it was also likely that they would not scruple at taking them wherever they could be found. It afterwards appeared that the Zulus had actually murdered, for the sake of their guns, four Dutchmen whom they found in a tent at some distance from their countrymen.

The review of the troops and narrative of the exploit at last ended, but other ceremonies following, the patience of Gardiner was severely tried by the delay to settle the boundary question. The triumphal dances at length were over. Dingarn was now ready to listen; he and his Indunas wanted more presents, but Gardiner positively refused to give any more. Dingarn and the Indunas retired, and after a short interval Gardiner also returned to his hut. This had not been expected, and a message was therefore sent to know if he intended to go away without taking leave; another interview was, therefore, necessary, which ended in a friendly, but still unsatisfactory manner; and on the same day Gardiner set out for home.

But we must now accompany the Owens to Unkunginglove. Their journey from Hambanati thither lasted twenty days, and was accomplished in wagons, in a country without roads. They visited the American missionaries in the Clomanthleen district, and derived great encouragement from the fact that these missionaries had been allowed to remain there for eighteen months, and in that time had been able to acquire a considerable knowledge of the language. Mr. Owen made a point of inviting the natives to attend the services each Sunday. Seated on the ground, in order to render his discourse more familiar, he on one occasion taught a group of fifteen men. They were attentive, continually asking questions, not of the preacher, however, but of themselves. One old man, however, once desired them to be quiet and listen; but another told Mr. Owen that he talked first about one thing and then about another, so that they could not understand. On another Sunday, an Induna collected his people and brought them to the service. A conversational sermon was given them. The Induna asked some pointed questions; "Whether Jesus Christ had sent the preacher to them?" Mr. Owen replied, "that he had felt him in his heart, and that he knew his coming to teach them was pleasing to him." He further said, "that Jesus Christ had not spoken to my outward ear, but he had spoken to my heart." The Induna then said, "that he supposed that it would please Jesus Christ if they came to hear his words." "Most assuredly," was the reply, "but still more if they believed and practised them."

Dingarn also received the missionaries kindly, and with his Indunas was very inquisitive on a variety of subjects.

Missionary operations commenced with the attempt to teach the Zulu children to read; they came to school by the order of the despot himself, and showed great tractability, as well as quickness in acquiring the first rudiments of knowledge. After teaching them the letters from a card, Mr. Owen bade them kneel down and be as silent as possible. "He would now," he said, "teach them how to pray to God; and whilst doing so, it would be wrong to look about idly, or play, or talk." He then bade them repeat, after the interpreter, the Lord's prayer, which they did with the greatest gravity and quietness, showing an example that would shame many children in Christian lands.

Mr. Owen was not only busied with this anxious labour of Christian love; he endeavoured also to reach the heart of the fierce Dingarn, by reasoning with him, and inducing him to attend the Sunday services. "I have come," he said, "from the other side of the sea, to teach the people God's word. God's word commands people to be obedient to Kings and Indunas; and makes those who obey it good in every respect." "But," said Dingarn, "has God said that Kings and Indunas ought to learn his word?" "Certainly," was the reply;

"small and great, all are to learn it." But to the request that he, and his people, and Indunas would come and be taught, there was but one reply. "Speak to my Indunas. I can do nothing with them." Umthlella was therefore spoken to, but he could do nothing without Tambuza, and Tambuza was sick. Still matters were progressing favourably. Very interesting conversations were entered into by a few inquiring natives, who soon became familiar with the name of Christ. But before any results could be perceived, an unseen cloud was gathering over not only the mission, but Dingarn and all his tribe.

Sixteen days had hardly passed since Mr. Owen's location at Unkunkinglove, before he was summoned to read to Dingarn a letter which he had received from the emigrant Dutch Boers, who, having become dissatisfied with the English government, determined to emigrate northward, and, passing the British boundary, settle on some unoccupied land, and live under their own laws. They expressed their desire for peace and good understanding with the Zulus, but requested an assignment of unoccupied land within Dingarn's territory to be made over to them.

No effect resulted from this first despatch. The school continued. Dingarn himself learned to read the words which were written on the children's cards, and paid so much outward respect for the Sabbath, that he never sent for Mr. Owen on that day.

At length a detachment of the Boers, under the command of Mr. Retief, arrived. The result of this visit was to alarm Dingarn. Their guns, their horses, their bold bearing, discovered to him a power he both envied and feared. The ferocious chief showed them a war dance, and asked for a similar exhibition in return. They told him they would show him "how the Boers danced on horseback;" and when his visitors proceeded to go through the evolutions of a sham fight, the "dance on horseback" both amazed and alarmed him. For the present, however, he dissembled, and gave a general consent to their proposal to settle in his neighbourhood; but even then the deep cunning of the subtle savage was planning the doom of his unconscious victims. The Boers departed; the work of teaching went on, but it struck Mr. Owen that Dingarn's manner was altered. He now wanted teachers of the use of fire-arms, but not of God's word. He still allowed the Sunday preaching to go on, but the sermon passed into a cavilling dispute on the part of the chief and his Indunas. One of the American missionaries came to visit the station, and Mr. Owen returned with him, and remained absent for a week. Letters had, during this time, been received from Mr. Retief. He was employed to read them, but was not informed of any of Dingarn's intentions. He was not uneasy, and went on quietly fulfilling the duties of his mission, when one day he was startled from his security by the arrival of two messengers from Capt. Gardiner, urging him to be on his guard, as he had observed symptoms of treachery on the part of Dingarn, which might involve the safety of all the missionaries; and concluded by an offer of his own station as an asylum to all, if they should think it right to leave the Zulu country for a time.

Having now brought our narrative to the eve of the bursting of the storm, which swept away the Zulu mission, we must go back to view Capt. Gardiner's rising settlement at Hambanati.

A beautiful spot had been selected for the location of the new tribe, at an equal distance between Port Natal and the Tugala. The tent of the Gardiners had been exchanged for a thatched house. A rising ground, on which the huts of the natives now formed a village, was about a mile from the sea, and looked down on the river, winding among the hills and forest wood. Beautiful glens, which invited to retirement; trees standing in individual beauty or forming umbrageous woods; the steep banks of the Umtongata, fringed with an infinite variety of bushes occasionally hiding the course of the stream, presented a most beautiful combination of rich and varied scenery and tints of all colours. It was beautiful to behold. The unpretending house upon the hill, surrounded by a few huts, a primitive Zulu village on another hill, with Indian corn waving in all directions, an open sea view on the eastern side; in a northerly direction a steep hill arose from which the whole coast was visible as far as Port Natal, the point of which appeared to be nearly opposite, stretching far out into the sea.

This was Hambanati, which had advanced so rapidly from nature's wildness, that it seemed almost to have been a work of magic. The moral improvement was scarcely less rapid. The clothed tribe were increasing in numbers, and the men were faithful and seemed glad to be instructed. Captain Gardiner, wishing to send a letter to Bunting (a distance of one hundred miles), first asked one of them if he were afraid to go through a country belonging to other tribes. The native, pointing to the country of the greatest enemy of the Zulus, replied, "If you send me to Moselekatse, I will go."

Nothing could exceed the promise of this opening missionary establishment. The Scriptures were read, interpreted, and explained to those rude children of nature on every alternate morning; and on the succeeding one they were questioned upon the lesson. They were quite ready also to ask intelligent questions. During the day they were all occupied in different kinds of work, fencing, planting, and building. On Sunday the school was crowded; the men and women were instructed by questions and answers; the children were taught from Watts's Catechism in Zulu. Some of the girls learned to sew neatly, and became useful in domestic occupations.

Thus seven months passed peacefully over at

Hambanati; but the calm current was now to be interrupted. The year 1838 commenced amid great hopes for the future; the missionary pioneers were to be joined by Mr. and Mrs. Hewetson, sent out by the Church Missionary Society; but these hopeful prospects were destroyed by the irruption of the Dutch Boers.

We have already seen the threatening aspect of affairs, when the first detachment of Boers under Retief, demanded a tract of country from Dingarn. The Zulu chief feigned compliance with their request, and presented them with the tract he had formerly given to Lieutenant Farewell, and afterwards to Captain Gardiner, but only on condition of their recovering some cattle which had been carried off by the neighbouring tribe of Moselekatse. Retief consented, and the cattle were brought back and the requested territory was given. The same ceremonies had on a former occasion were repeated. Refreshments were offered to the Boers, and during the performance of a war dance, the unsuspecting witnesses were gradually surrounded by a large circle formed by the whole body of Zulus. Wheeling slowly and remorselessly round them, the circle narrowed, when, on a preconcerted signal, a rush was made, the trusting Dutch were seized, dragged out, and dispatched on the spot.

So suddenly was this horrible deed performed, that, until the moment of the massacre, Mr. Owen had not even a suspicion of any foul play. Retief had breakfasted with him and had spoken highly of Dingarn. The first notice he received of this black treachery, was from the chief himself, who sent him a message, "not to fear. He had killed the Boers because they had plotted against him, but he would not hurt Mr. Owen." There was little confidence to be placed in this assurance; but having with his family passed a day of fearful uncertainty, they found comfort in their evening worship, by reading the ninety-first Psalm: "A thousand shall fall beside thee; and ten thousand at thy right hand; but it shall not come nigh thee." As they witnessed large bodies of Dingarn's army move rapidly in the direction of the Tugala, they had little doubt but that another massacre was intended. The supposition was only too true; the Zulus rushed like a whirlwind on the camp of the Dutch emigrants, and killed upwards of one hundred and fifty men, women, and children.

As it was now certain that no trust could be placed on Dingarn's word, the Owens left Unkunginglove, and after a toilsome journey reached Hambanati. Spending one night only with the Gardiners, they resumed, on the following day, their journey to Port Natal, where they arrived just in time to receive Mr. and Mrs. Hewetson on their landing.

The Gardiners remained one week longer to watch the progress of events. But when the inhabitants of Natal determined to join the Dutch in an exterminating war against the Zulus, they took their leave of Hambanati, sorrowful but resigned. Before he left, however, Captain Gardiner called his people together, and promised to use his utmost endeavours to find another country where they might settle in peace; provided they, on their side, would promise to take no part in the ensuing war. They promised, but the love of plunder and adventure caused one after another to join in the conflict; many lost their lives, and all lost their name as a tribe. One only remained faithful to his word. This was Umpondombeni, the first Zulu who became servant to Captain Gardiner. He attended him in each of his earlier visits to Dingarn, and welcomed him on the beach at Natal on his return from England. More recently we are told of his baptism and conversion to Christianity, as well as of his inconsolable grief on hearing of his master's death; proving that Gardiner's labours among the Zulus were not altogether in vain.

Umkonto, another interesting character among the Africans, was greatly attached to Gardiner, and paid great attention to the religious instruction given at Hambanati. But he, too, went to the war, and was one of the very few who escaped with life. Many years after, meeting with a gentleman going to England, begged him say to "Cappan Garna, that he promised to come again, if his hair was as white as his shirt, and tell him too, we are waiting for him." This message, as well as a little calabash which he brought, and had been used as a snuff-box, was accordingly faithfully delivered to Captain Gardiner, who, in return, sent a letter and a present to both these men, urging upon them his earnest request that they would go to a missionary station, and listen to the words of the Bible, which would make them happy for ever.

Seeing the course which events were taking,—the Dutch at war with the Zulus, and his own men joining in the war,—Captain Gardiner determined to conduct his family away from the scene of strife. They sailed for Algoa Bay, with all the American missionaries, except one, who went to the Dutch camp.

Mr. Owen and Mr. Hewetson remained for a short time at Natal, in hopes of being able to renew the mission; but, with their families, soon after followed their friends to the colony.

Captain Gardiner did not remain long at Algoa Bay. He knew that many English and American missionaries would be on the watch to avail themselves of the first safe opportunity to return to Port Natal. He, the missionary pioneer, considered that many years, in all likelihood, must elapse before the Zulu country could again be open to missionaries; and, altogether unconscious of the great exertions friends at home were making to support his plans at Hambanati, he felt himself called to leave South Africa for ever.

So intricate are human affairs! In going in advance of the colony to endeavour to plant a mission among the Zulus, Captain Gardiner had succeeded beyond his hope. He had obtained a grant of land, and permission for Zulus to assemble round him as their chief, and settle on that tract of land. He brought out his family, and formed a new tribe around him, by whose friendly aid missionaries passed northward into the very heart of the Zulu country. Zulu schools were formed, Zulu boys were learning to read, and Zulu girls were being taught the employments belonging to civilized life.

This was all counteracted by the failure to settle the old boundary question, which had first led to the Kafir war, in which the Dutch suffered so severely. This it was that induced the Boers to emigrate northward, and having heard that Dingarn had already granted land to Gardiner, they determined that either by treaty or force he should grant land to them also. Then followed the march of ten thousand farmers, the advance of Retief's party of one thousand; their recovery of Dingarn's cattle, followed by Dingarn's treachery; war between the Dutch and the Zulus; in the midst of which the Zulu mission and Captain Gardiner's tribe were swept away.

For a time it appeared as if the whole scheme had been a failure. But Captain Gardiner was only a little in advance of the day. No glimpse of hearty co-operation from home assisted him in all these perplexing circumstances, which, as a missionary pioneer, he bravely encountered alone.

Twenty years have passed since the events just narrated have occurred, and great are the changes wrought by their passage. Another Kafir war has resulted in the establishment of a safer frontier. Port Natal is made a colony, a town has been built there, a church is in progress, and large numbers of English settlers have gone there. Many of the Dutch have resumed their allegiance, the Zulu power is broken up, Dingarn, who assassinated his elder brother Charka, has himself been destroyed by his younger brother, Umpanda, who has succeeded him as chief. Instead of two thousand, the Zulu refugees now number one hundred thousand. Three of the American missionaries have returned to their posts, and have flourishing stations, and a printing press. Wesleyan missionaries have followed, and more recently an English bishop with a staff of clergy.

Thus, the plans of man may fail, but the Lord Omnipotent reigns, and acknowledges the smallest efforts which are made in his service.

CHAPTER VI.

SOUTH AMERICA. 1838–1839.

"Which now of these three, thinkest thou, was neighbour unto him that fell among the thieves? And he said, He that showed mercy on him. Then said Jesus unto him, Go, and do thou likewise.—LUKE x. 36, 37.

VIEWING his own life as dedicated to those among the heathen who had been left uncared for by other Christian efforts, Gardiner now turned his thoughts to South America, the scene of his boyish travels, and the continent which, from his personal knowledge, he knew to be, perhaps more than any other, fast bound in the chains of misery and iron bondage. The transient gleams of light, that had occasionally broken in upon its darkness, had faded almost as rapidly as they arose.

Where there was peace, popery was dominant, and ready to crush out every spark that might be kindled by the gospel light. Where war was going forward, so strong a prejudice against Europeans generally possessed the Indian mind, that there seemed no hope of obtaining even a patient hearing from them.

This was not to be wondered at. All who have read the story of the mighty struggle by which the conquest of Peru and Chili was effected, must abhor the treachery of the conquerors, and sympathize with the victims. What has the religion of Rome, as taught by the conquerors, done for the brave race whose allegiance they demanded to God and the Pope, when they seized the land and enslaved its owners? The natives have had continued cause to say, in the words of one of Pizarro's victims, "They did not understand the religion of the white men."

The fury with which the early Portuguese settlers hunted down the natives for slaves, the severity with which they treated those whom they retained, and the recklessness with which they sold the remainder, are matters of history. The Jesuits, indeed, by a mild treatment and moderate instruction, endeavoured and succeeded in attracting the natives in crowds to their mission stations; but incurring the hatred of the Portuguese of the colony of St. Paul, they were driven away, and their settlement destroyed.

The Jesuits are not easily baffled. They founded mission stations on the rivers Paraguay and Uruguay, which flourished there for one hundred and fifty years. They treated the natives with humanity, partly civilized and instructed them, taught them various trades, but made them thoroughly dependent on their teachers for subsistence as well as instruction.

There was always an impassable gulf between them. The Jesuit was born and remained a superior; the native was born an inferior, and could never rise. The Jesuit occupied the throne; the native sat on the footstool. Giving offence to the government by interfering with politics, they were banished from Paraguay in 1767, by order of Charles III., king of Spain. Left without guides of any kind, the Indians relapsed into barbarism. They were like children who had never been taught to run alone; and were so dependent on their masters that they could do nothing for themselves.

All this was known to Gardiner, and as he paced the deck of the schooner, which was carrying him and his family to Rio Janeiro, his heart was filled with compassion for the wronged red men of the South.

Was there a fatality, he asked within himself, by which the bold South American Indians were always to be deprived of their teachers? Had the Europeans nothing to give them but war or slavery? Are the sickly shores of the Essequibo, and the swamps of British Guayana, the only spots open to Protestant missions? Are no other efforts to be made to carry the message of an offered pardon to the innumerable natives of the other parts of the South American continent? Will no one try to speak a kindly word to them for Christ's sake? Will no one explore the way to those heathen tribes who are being left in darkness and heathenism, to grow daily more savage and fierce? The answer of his benevolent heart, to these communings, may be easily imagined. He determined to shun no toil, to shrink from no danger, in his persevering efforts to obtain a channel for the living waters, in this arid spiritual desert. What was peril, fatigue, privation, in comparison with effecting the cause that lay nearest his heart—namely—to break the bread of life to the perishing heathen of South America?

After a detention of three weeks at Rio, Captain Gardiner embarked with his family for Monte Video, from whence they went to Buenos Ayres, where they found the port blockaded by a squadron of French ships. The packet was, however, allowed to enter. The usual mode of landing here, is to be transferred from a ship to a boat, and from the boat to a cart, which has been driven into the water. In this cart the passengers and baggage are conveyed with many a jerk to the shore, and deposited on the beach. A few peons were soon found to carry the bags, and the family followed them on foot. They had not long been in comfortable quarters, which he had much difficulty to obtain, before a pampero, or sweeping wind from the Pampas, set in, with torrents of rain. These pamperos generally last about three days, and during this time the city appears like a scene of desolation. The neighbouring district being low, it soon becomes a swamp, when, with water below and wind above, neither men nor beasts can keep their feet; even the milk-sellers and market people do not enter the city at such times. The effect is, nevertheless, refreshing; for, when the clouds recede, all nature smiles, the country traders come in, the city pours forth its tide of busy life, and the ground becomes dry with marvellous rapidity.

The Gardiners received much kindness from several of their countrymen; but, becoming acquainted with the British chaplain and his family, spent the last week of their stay with them. The Rev. John Armstrong had been several years resident at Buenos Ayres and entered heartily into all Captain Gardiner's plans and projects. He considered the Spanish Americans to be a fine race of people, who only wanted the advantage of a settled government and a pure religion. For the Indians of the Pampas, nothing could be done in this quarter; there was no access to them from Buenos Ayres, while the present exterminating system of warfare continued. On one occasion eighty Indians were brought captive into the city, and by the order of General Rosas, shot by tens in the market place.

The vast tribes of Indians to the northward were reported to live more peaceably, cultivating the ground and weaving their own cloth. Most of these, it was said, spoke the Guayrani, a language which had been reduced to writing by the Jesuits, and called by them, "La lingua general," from its being spoken over such an extent of country.

Captain Gardiner decided on an immediate journey to Mendoza with the intention of proceeding thence to the Indians of Chili, although told that to cross the mountains at this season of the year was impracticable. He thought, however, he should make better progress in Spanish where there were few opportunities of speaking English, and be better able to prosecute his inquiries into the state of the Indians on the frontier.

On the 10th of August, therefore, he took passage in a galera, or kind of Buenos Ayrean omnibus, packed with portmanteaus and cases, drawn by five mounted horses, and with a courier in advance, took the direction of the Pampas. The passengers, four in number, carried with them such things as are necessary for cooking, and mattrasses for sleeping, in the galera. The roads were bad, but the horses were swift and powerful. As they approached Luxan, the rain came down in torrents, and the galera was, by no means, water-tight. But travellers become fertile in expedients. Captain Gardiner drilled holes in the floor of the galera, and let the water run off.

Rapid travelling is, indeed, necessary across the Pampas, for fear of attacks from the mounted Indians who often appear in the distance, like a herd of wild horses. Lying in an almost horizontal position, they cannot be distinguished from the animals to which they cling, until, on approaching the object of attack, they suddenly leap upright. It may then easily be imagined with what interest the traveller would eye every moving speck in the distance on these never-ending plains, and how the peons would quicken the pace of their horses, as they passed over the more dangerous portions of the road. The poor hovels of post-houses, with their unswept earth floors and scanty, ill-kept furniture, offered small temptation for the travellers to linger; but, in this fine climate, they found this to be an inconvenience only at night. Many of these post-houses are surrounded with a deep trench, and an interior hedge of cactus; this, being doubled, constitutes an impregnable defence in Indian warfare; the Gardiners, however, were much surprised to find many of these post-houses entirely destitute of any fence or protection. Between Repusa and the Desaguadero, the first view of the Cordilleras was obtained, as they hid their snowy summits in the clouds. The river was passed with some difficulty, the principal contents of the galera were ferried over on a raft, floated by six empty casks; the galera itself being dragged through the river by the half-scrambling, half-swimming horses. In fourteen days, not including Sundays, they had passed over nine hundred miles of Pampas, and found themselves comfortably settled in the country-house of General Aldao, within two miles of Mendoza, where they were hospitably allowed to remain, until the proper time for crossing the Cordillera.

The result of all Captain Gardiner's inquiries soon showed the hopelessness of any attempt to visit the Indians from thence. Five years previous, a combined force had taken the field against some turbulent tribes, and all the prisoners taken were shot. This barbarity became the established precedent. Many among the white population, although professing to abhor cruelty, found it hard to believe "that God has made of one blood all nations of men for to dwell on all the face of the earth," so our indefatigable pioneer found not one to bid him "God speed," in the work on which his heart was set.

In Mendoza the Bible is not prohibited by law, but is generally discountenanced by the priests. One of the principal booksellers agreed to place some Bibles and Testaments, which Gardiner supplied him with, in his shop, but he returned them in a few days, declaring they were unsaleable.

Gratuitous distribution was now resorted to, and the house was besieged with applicants. One morning before breakfast, twenty-two women and children came to ask for Bibles. The stock was soon exhausted, though no one received a book without being required to read a verse to prove his ability to do so.

On the 12th of October, our friends left Mendoza to begin their difficult journey across the Cordillera. A long cavalcade of mules and horses, with a sufficient number of arrieros, carried the travellers and their baggage. The children travelled in panniers, newly invented for the occasion, instead of being seated, as was the ordinary mode, on a pillow in front of a mounted peon. After a fatiguing ride through a rocky and broken country, almost compensated for by scenes of wild, melancholy grandeur, they found a most acceptable resting-place at Uzpallata, in the last inhabited house on the Mendoza side of the mountains, where they spent the Sabbath. On the fourth day, they reached the "Bad Pass," which all travellers represent as requiring great steadiness and some nerve to venture over, as the stones are loosened by the pressure of each footstep, and roll down into the stream which roars below. The next day they reached the "Inca's bridge," which consists of a natural arch with a span of eighty or ninety feet, formed by a sulphureous spring.

Steeper and steeper became the toilsome path as the cavalcade approach the Cumbre. The tired horses could hardly move along without their burdens, therefore all the party walked except the children. But all fatigue was forgotten when they reached the glorious summit; horses, mules, and men, all were alike equally tired, and, for the moment, equally happy.

The grand sea of snow, which extended thirteen miles on the Chilian side of the Cumbre, was unnoticed. Captain and Mrs. Gardiner walked the first six miles to a rest-house, where they passed the night. An impromptu palanquin was contrived for the children. These rest-houses, valuable relics of the Spanish rule, are formed "entirely of brick, with a coped roof of the same material, supported by an arch which forms the ceiling: they contain but one room, which is entered by a flight of steep steps, the floors being raised about six feet from the foundation, to allow for the drifting of the snow in winter." The change in the scenery on the descent was marked and beautiful, varied as it was with every natural charm. Silvery cascades, broken fragments of rock, with trees and shrubs, pleased the eye; and some signs of cultivation, and the habitations of man, which appeared here and there, poor as they were, gave a humanizing air to the landscape.

They reached the foot of the mountains in eight days after leaving Mendoza. Three days later found them at Santiago, from which place they travelled on horseback through beautiful valleys, bounded by the snowy Cordillera. At night, the accommodation varied greatly, the travellers sometimes resting in a noisy inn, sometimes at a private dwelling, and sometimes at a wretched kind of outhouse, which afforded only shelter and privacy. At Talca they spent the Sunday in a comfortable inn, but the incessant crowing of cocks, and noise made by the cock-fighters assembled there, sent them to the neighbouring common for quiet and worship.

Many chasms and cracks in the soil at Talca and Chillan gave melancholy evidence of the recent earthquake of 1835, but at Concepcion the ruin had been so complete that three years seemed to have done little towards restoring it. The wide streets exhibited many vacancies; a row of houses, then a ruin, then perhaps a single house, while churches still lay prostrate, and only showed their former splendour by the extent of ground which their fragments covered. At the period of that awful earthquake, not a house was left standing. Yet the new structures now rising were of the same material, brick only, with a framework of wood. During the five weeks' stay of the Gardiners at Concepcion, they felt three shocks of earthquake, and wondered at the temerity of the builders, who continued their work, hoping, (as they said,) "that the new buildings would last their time." But are not each and all such instances but living commentaries upon more fatal and far less excusable presumption?

From previous information, Captain Gardiner anticipated easy intercourse from this place with the independent Indians. He understood that the Biobio was the boundary between the two nations, and that a friendly understanding existed between them. He had now to learn the fallacy of his hopes.

Leaving his family at Concepcion, he commenced his journey along the banks of the Biobio; and after four days travelling, arrived at San Carlos, one hundred miles from Concepcion. A servant rode a second horse, and led two others, which were loaded with the necessary baggage. The current of the Biobio is very rapid, and to cross it, a very primitive raft was constructed, consisting of four trunks of trees, lashed together by hide thongs to two poles, one at each end. When the whole party who were to cross were balanced on this machine, but one inch remained above the surface of the water. One of Captain Gardiner's horses was harnessed to the raft by knotting his tail with the tow rope. A boy leaped upon his back, and grasping the single lock of the mane which is left to grow, urged the frightened horse to swim with the unusual load in his rear.

After crossing two more rivers, they arrived at Piligen, where the first person they saw was Corbalan, the chief. He was on horseback, and wore a dark coloured poncho. He received them civilly, and ordered a sheep to be killed and dressed for supper. The house was of an oval form, and about thirty-five feet long, with wattled side walls about five feet high. The floor was of mud, and the roof neatly thatched with grass. The fire-place was in the centre, and here the supper was cooked.

Corbalan, being informed of the motives of this visit, namely, a desire to learn the language, and teach his people a knowledge of the true God, although he thought the proposal a strange one, made no objection, but, after a little further explanation, seemed cordially to enter into it. As he spoke Spanish, it was agreed he should teach Gardiner his own language, and in return be instructed in the word of God. He expressed great willingness to see the Book in which God has taught men respecting himself, and the way to heaven. "It was good," he said, "and he should be glad." When asked what were his ideas of the condition of the soul after the death of the body, he acknowledged that they were all in ignorance on that point; some believing that it lived in another world, while others supposed that it ceased to exist.

Notice had been sent over night to the neighbouring chiefs to assemble their people, to welcome the arrival of the white strangers; and in the morning as soon as Corbalan and his guest were mounted, the former led the way to the group which was collected under the trees near his house. Some mounted their horses, others were on foot, but all advanced, and in turn came up and shook hands. Corbalan apologized for the smallness of the party, which amounted to forty-five men, saying that the greater part of his people were absent in the mountains. Five inferior chiefs were, however, among them, two of whom, in passing, presented Gardiner with a boiled fowl. He was rather puzzled to know where to bestow this unexpected token of their friendship; the interpreter, however, relieved him of his dilemma by cramming them in his saddle-bags.

A suitable present, some coloured cotton handkerchiefs, and a few brass buttons, were distributed among the chiefs, to which some indigo and beads were added. The gifts intended for Corbalan had been presented on the preceding night.

This was but a transient vision of success; at the next meeting with Corbalan, Gardiner found that his mind had undergone a great change.

On returning from a ride with the friendly chief, Gardiner pointed out a spot suitable for a mission-house, but no sooner was the subject named, than Corbalan declared that, notwithstanding what he had before said, he must now withdraw his consent. The reasons which he assigned for this unexpected refusal, were, in all probability, the result of a conference with the chiefs, and seemed sufficiently weighty. Although desirous that Gardiner should remain, he said that it would not be safe; the Huilliches, a large and warlike tribe, would be offended if a foreigner lived so near them. As soon as they heard it, they would attack him, and he should not be able to resist.

Much disappointed, Captain Gardiner took leave of this spot, which had awakened a deep interest in his devoted heart, and returned to Concepcion, where he remained only three days before setting out for Arauco, where he determined to make an attempt to conciliate the Indians of that district. But, although hospitably entertained by the commandant, he was assured that there was no likelihood of his being permitted to proceed into the Indian territory; a French naturalist, M. Gay, had made the attempt very recently, and been compelled to return. A chain of forts were formerly established from Concepcion to Chiloe, intended to keep the natives in check, and in every fort missionaries were stationed. At one time there were twenty-five of these stations, but the Indians eyed them with jealousy, and hated the soldier without loving the priest. But in 1810, when the Chilians had thrown off their allegiance to Spain, they made overtures to the Indians for aid, and the latter were not slow to learn their importance, and to wish for independence. Joining their forces with those under the command of a renegade freebooter, named Benavides, they recovered so great an amount of power, that the Chilians discovered that the day of their mastery was gone. They, therefore, adopted a new policy, and at the time of Captain Gardiner's visit had established friendly relations with many of the frontier chiefs, of whom Corbalan was one. Many of these chiefs received presents and annual pay from the government; others, however, refused all overtures, and despised those who had entered into the pay of their late enemies. Thus jealousies and quarrels subsisted among themselves, and the frontier tribes, who were not above receiving Chilian pay, formed a barrier between Chili and the more remote and powerful tribes.

The Huilliches had refused to enter into this treaty, and therefore it was that Corbalan, the chief of a less powerful tribe under Chilian influence, dared not, for fear of the Huilliche people, admit Captain Gardiner for more than a passing visit.

Commissaries were stationed in the neighbourhood of all the friendly tribes, to prevent or facilitate interviews with them, as the case might be. If a stranger visited a chief, the question would be asked, "Have you brought a pass from the commissary?" and if he first applied to a commissary, it would most likely be inquired, "What is your business with the chief?" Another hindrance to our missionary pioneer's advancing among the independent tribes, was their keen recollection of the forts as mission stations, and hatred of soldiers and priests, and it was only by the subtle policies of the latter, that they could ever obtain audience with the chiefs.

Disappointed, but not discouraged, from the pursuit of his great object, Gardiner retraced his steps to Concepcion, and soon afterwards transported his family to Valdivia where, believing him to be a naturalist, he was called El Botanico, and birds and insects were daily offered him for sale.

The neighbouring Indians were said to be all free and independent; but by slow degrees the discovery was made that this independence included Chilian pay and Chilian influence, except when it assumed so hostile a bearing that no intercourse was tolerated but under the most rigorous restrictions. Captain Gardiner, therefore, after making a short exploring journey alone, conducted his family to Quinchilca, where they were to remain until he made a further exploration.

Although the distance allotted for this day's journey was not more than twenty-five miles, there were so many delays before the animals were collected and in readiness to start, and the road so difficult, that night overtook them; and the guide, who owned the whole cavalcade of horses, declared it impracticable to proceed farther. He would not, therefore, listen to any remonstrances, but coolly gave Gardiner the choice between an Indian house on one side of the road, and an apple-tree on the other, as a suitable halting-place for his family. The walls of the house were made of squared trunks of trees, placed side by side, and set upright in the ground. The summer's sun had its usual effect upon the wood, and chinks and open crevices obviated any need for windows. Seeing through some of these openings that the house was full of Indians, little desire was felt to enter it. But as there was no alternative, they ventured, and found no reason to regret the adventure. The buzz of conversation was at once hushed, and a raised platform in one corner was instantly vacated and offered to the strangers. One by one, the inmates silently left the house, leaving only the women, who were cooking the evening meal, and some children. When this operation was over, the savoury mess was shared with the visitors, and bread received in return.

After arranging as far as possible for the comfort

of his family, Gardiner left them at Quinchilca, and resumed his travels. It was difficult to find an interpreter, but he procured a man who was willing to do his best, and proceeded on horseback to the Indian territory. After crossing the river Callecalle six times, and another, whose banks were covered with a jungle of bamboo, (from which the Indians made their spears,) they found themselves near to Lake Ranco, and in the village of Neggiman, one of the paid chiefs, with whom Gardiner had a satisfactory interview. The question was asked, "May I come and reside at your village with my family?" The answer was, "Oh yes, certainly; that is, if you bring me a letter from Don Francisco, the commissary." Gardiner was delighted: he had met Don Francisco, and knew that he would make no difficulty. But he did not know Friar Manuel, of Valdivia, who, arriving at the commissary house, heard that El Botanico, an Englishman and a heretic, was desirous of settling in the Indian territory. "You surely will not give him permission," said the friar, "he will infect all the Indians with heresy, and set them against us." This argument prevailed over the friendly disposition of the commissary; but desirous of pleasing both the stranger and the priest, he wrote a civil letter to the chief, and sent it by a civil messenger, who at the same time delivered a private message, the purport of which Gardiner gathered from his next interview with Neggiman, who inquired, "How long do you think of remaining here?" The reply was, "that as he wished to learn the language, and to become acquainted with the people, it would occupy at least twelve moons." To this the chief rejoined, that his visitor "might stay one moon and no more." It was easy to see that the chief had been tampered with, but it was not until a later period that Gardiner found out by whose influence his benevolent views had been thwarted.

Neggiman's whole tone and bearing being altered, there seemed but one hope left. As nothing could be done with the chiefs who received government pay, Gardiner determined to visit the Huilliches, a tribe of men really independent.

Provided with a fresh guide and a good horse, he pursued a fatiguing journey, mostly through a thick jungle of bamboo, and with torn skin and tattered clothes, reached the Indian territory. The neat cottages, with patches of barley and potatoes, and the distant roaring of the sea, gave a most refreshing change to the scene.

Ushered into the presence of the chief, Wykepang, a stout, elderly man, Gardiner was asked, "Where are you going?" "I wish to go forward and visit some of the Huilliche chiefs beyond." Wykepang laughed, and said, "There are no Spaniards there; they are not allowed to come there." Gardiner contrived however to make him understand he was no intruder, and told him he "had come for no other purpose than to instruct him and his people in the Book of God. Wykepang seemed surprised that his visitor should possess the Book of God, but when the word "missionary" was named, all his prejudice against everything Spanish came out, and he replied quickly, that "he did not want a missionary." After many questions to the guide, for he was very suspicious that his guest belonged to Buenos Ayres, the chief gave an unwilling permission that he might stay one night, adding that all the chiefs of the Huilliches had agreed never to allow Spaniards to enter their country.

At a very early hour in the morning Wykepang reminded his guest that it was time to go, and that it must not be known that a foreigner had slept in his house. On departing, Gardiner asked his host, "When I pay you another visit, if I can speak your language instead of the Spanish, what am I to expect?" "Then," said he, "you may come without fear."

With this partial permission, our friend took his leave, and after a return journey, made up of hardships and mishaps, he reached Quinchilca, from which he immediately removed his family to Valdivia. Thus, thwarted and disappointed in every effort, Allen Gardiner saw no hope remaining of getting at the heathen in South America. Fierce, exterminating warfare, in some parts, led the Indian to look on every Christian as his enemy. Whereever peace reigned, Popery was dominant, and Protestant teaching was unwelcome.

But his energies were not to be crushed by failure, and he looked about for some other work on which to expend them. There was still a large unoccupied field in South America, where neither the Bible nor Tract Societies had a single agent, and the idea struck him that they would willingly grant him books, and that he might act for both. His decision was soon made. "No!" said he, "I have devoted myself to God, to seek for openings among the heathen, and I cannot go back or modify my vow."

From this resolution he never swerved; and looking at the map of the world as another man might look at that of Europe or England, he thought as little of going to the antipodes, as a Philadelphian would of going to Boston. He therefore determined to visit the Indian Archipelago, and accordingly, on May 29th, 1839, with his family, set sail from Valparaiso for Sydney.

CHAPTER VII.

THE INDIAN ARCHIPELAGO.

"From many a palmy plain,
They call us to deliver
Their land from error's chain."

AFTER a fortnight's boisterous weather, for want of a good chart, the vessel in which he sailed made a wrong passage among the Society Islands, and found it necessary to put in at Tahiti. They found this island, once a land of promise, then a land of trouble, fast degenerating from the excellent example of a Christian people, for which it had been remarkable. After the delay of a few days, the vessel again weighed anchor, and on Sept. 14th, reached Sydney Cove, from which place he determined to proceed to New Guinea. On hearing that the Romanist Bishop of Sydney was himself projecting a mission to that country, he engaged a passage to Timor, in the hope of obtaining permission from the Dutch Protestant authorities, to open a mission. "What an example of zeal these Romanists set us!" was Gardiner's thought, as he paced the deck of the vessel whilst she wound her dangerous way through the difficult passages of the Barrier Reef and Torres Strait, on her course to Timor.

As they approached that port, Captain Gardiner began to hear alarming accounts of Dutch restrictions, which, when a trial was made, he found were not without foundation. On Oct. 23d, they arrived at Dille, where they were kindly received by the Governor, who, having retired to the hills for health, kindly allowed the use of the government house, whilst they remained in this unhealthy place. The Gardiners were detained three weeks before any opportunity for leaving occurred. It seemed as if to breathe the air were poison, and sickness was imprinted on the faces of all. During their stay, Gardiner was as active as ever, adding to his information from every quarter, both as to the European settlements and position, and the character of the natives.

Having made a pleasant acquaintance with the Padre, a Dominican friar who could speak French and Spanish, the two friends, mounted on the sturdy little ponies of Timor, went together to visit some of the mountain villages. The way led through dark ravines, and up the steep ascent of the first ridge of mountains; the Padre, however, was a good travelling companion, and the weary miles were cheated of their length by his conversation. He stated, that great difficulties lay in the way of intercourse with the natives, from the variety of dialects in use among them, and this was afterwards confirmed by an intelligent native, who represented each tribe as speaking a language of its own, and the various chiefs to be independent of each other. The natives of Timor are of a dark chocolate colour, with lamp-black hair, and wear a single garment of home manufacture.

This discouragement, together with the unhealthiness of the climate, of which his family were beginning to feel the sickening effects, convinced Captain Gardiner that further research would, at this time, be useless, and therefore, having an opportunity of obtaining a passage to Copang, he embarked with them for that place, taking with them a native servant named Manoko. From this time they suffered greatly from intermittent fever, but were, by God's mercy, never wholly laid aside.

After sailing for three days along a line of coast most picturesque and beautiful, but with the same poisoned air sweeping around them and filling their sails, they reached Copang. Gardiner found the Dutch Resident kind and civil, but the latter was much surprised at the request for a pass, and the project of a mission to Papua. He said he had no objection to give the English stranger the requisite pass, but that he might as well attempt to instruct the monkeys as the natives of Papua. "Monkeys in appearance or not," said Gardiner, "being men in reality, they are not incapable of being instructed, for they are included in our Saviour's command, to preach the gospel to every human being."

Finding a comfortable country-house, situated in a delightful grove of trees, cocoanut, canary, and banana, he settled his family there; whilst he, in spite of the severe attacks of fever he suffered on every alternate day, prosecuted the object of his visit with his usual untiring activity. In this he received much assistance from a Dutch missionary.

"Either for want of funds, or energy, or both, a sad clog seems to impede the operations of the Dutch Missionary Society among these islands. Notwithstanding that eleven years have elapsed since the society at Rotterdam first commenced its missions in these seas, but one translation of the Scriptures exists for the whole native population, from Malacca to Timor and the Moluccas; nor is any other in progress. This translation is in the purest Malay, which widely differs from the colloquial tongue of by far the greater portion of countries within the range of the Society's operations. The clergyman at Copang preaches in Malay, but his auditors generally are unable to comprehend a great part of his discourse. Mr. Heimering informs me that, during his residence as missionary at the island of Letti, he found it so utterly impracticable to make any progress through the medium of Malay, which was but imperfectly understood by a portion of the population, that soon after his arrival he set himself down to study the native tongue, which he at length acquired. He then commenced translating some elementary books, the four Gospels, and the Acts, into the language of Letti, supposing that his Society would, of course, print them, and thereby facilitate his labours. But this they have wholly declined, under the plea, that the population, for the benefit of which they were intended, was too small to warrant the expense. The population of Letti alone is computed by Mr. Heimering at ten thousand, and, if it were less, the general question would not be affected by it; especially as the translation would bear upon thirty or forty thousand persons, who inhabit islands of the same group. Now, when it is considered that the entire population of Tahiti, where six missionaries are labouring, is not yet quite ten thousand, and that printing-presses are in operation in all the adjacent groups, where there has been found a distinct dialect, it does seem almost unaccountable that the all-important work of translation has not been even commenced by the Dutch Society, with reference to these poor islanders."

Mr. Heimering, however, informed him that without a knowledge of the native tongue, his project would prove to be impracticable.

It must here be remarked, that although the Malays are now known only as the pirates of the Indian Archipelago, they are the original inhabitants of the Malayan peninsula and the island of Sumatra. In many of these islands there are two coloured races, besides a few Europeans. The one race has more of the negro characteristics than the other, and are always found in the mountainous parts.

New Guinea is peopled entirely by blacks. The Dutch had at one time a settlement on the coast, called Fort du Bus, but that had been given up, and there was now no communication between any of the Dutch settlements and New Guinea.

Notwithstanding these obstacles, Gardiner still resolved to see for himself, determined to proceed to Ternate, hoping to take advantage of the influence of the Resident of Ternate over the Sultan of Tidore, and through that of the latter over the natives of New Guinea, through the island of Salawatty.

Although he was in such ill-health as to be unable to superintend the equipments of his voyage, he chartered a cutter and embarked on Dec. 27th for Ternate. It was at the time when the westerly monsoon was blowing, the vessel was in a wretched state, and with an ignorant pilot to guide her, was not only run far out of her course, but in danger of being wrecked. At length the bay of Solor was reached; and the ship's company spent New Year's day, 1840, at the Malay town of Lamkara, where they were detained until the vessel could be refitted and supplies be obtained.

This detention afterwards proved to be providential. Before they were ready to sail, news arrived that the north entrance of the Flores straits was occupied by a number of Malay pirates, who were on the watch for vessels. Many stories of piratical treatment to European ships were largely discussed among the passengers; which accounts being confirmed by a Portuguese padre on board, Captain Gardiner resolved to alter his course. That he regarded this escape from danger as providential, may be seen by an entry made in his journal:—

"It was, indeed, a most gracious Providence which directed us to this place. Had we obtained the supplies we needed, in sufficient quantity, at Solor, we should have run through the straits without in the least suspecting our danger, and, if becalmed within sight of land, should undoubtedly have been attacked by these merciless pirates. Had we been manned by Europeans, and properly armed, I should have had no hesitation in running through, small as our vessel was; but the two guns we had mounted would not have been of the slightest use."

Instead, therefore, of proceeding to Ternate, for, although he could not throw off the fever, he never thought of returning while any hope of success remained, he sailed for Amboyna, where he had an interview with the governor. His plans and objects excited both curiosity and surprise. The governor did not seem suspicious about his reasons for visiting New Guinea, and nothing transpired as to any meditated obstacle; but like a cautious general, this functionary formed his plan and acted upon it in silence.

The Gardiners found the settlement at Amboyna

a perfect forest of fruit trees. Every house was in a grove or plantation of bread-fruit, shaddock, mango, banana, nutmeg, and cinnamon,—for every species of spice and fruit seemed to luxuriate here—and over the door of every house sat a red parrot, like a sentinel on duty. The natives only are the cultivators of spices; they are required to send their produce to the governor at set prices. For their own food, sago is so easily cultivated that the natives find it too much trouble to grow anything else. But the "spicy breezes" so boasted of by voyagers, "although," says Gardiner, "the wind was directly off shore, as we approached the anchorage, regaled us not with their fragrance. I have never experienced it in the least degree, even when close to the island of Ceylon, where, if it ever were to be perceived, it would be in its perfection."

The Gardiners left Amboyna on Feb. 24th, and, embarking on board a vessel bound for Java, they found a motley company on board. They represented England; their servant was a native of Timor; some of the sailors were Americans, and a Dane and Javanese were among the passengers. The Captain was an Arab, the crew Malays, the cook a Chinaman; and the bows of the vessel were crimson with parrots. The Mohamedan element in this assembly contributed to render this passage unpleasant. Christians must eat; but the Mohamedans were intolerant as to their cooking-stove.

Manoko, the Gardiners' Timor servant, waited near the stove till the Arabs and Malays were supplied with food; but found that Mohamedans could not allow their cook to assist infidel Christians, nor would they hurry their movements, that the despised race might help themselves. The Gardiners were thus instructed in patience, and Manoko in cookery.

As the vessel approached her destination, the glasses were raised, and every eye was turned in the direction of the welcome land. The passengers pointed out to each other the position of the town, but no town was visible. The ship entered the harbour. Here an extraordinary scene of desolation presented itself. Shattered and unroofed houses were to be seen in every direction; not a dwelling of brick or stone was standing; the whole place had the appearance of a huge quarry in complete disorder, with wooden tenements here and there, as though they were the abodes of workmen in the midst of their materials.

The story was soon told. An eruption of the volcano of Ternate had taken place a month before, and for two days a stream of lava flowed, with some intermission, down the side of the mountain. For ten days after this all was quiet; then in the dead of night, the inhabitants were roused by the first shock of an earthquake. The shocks increased in violence until four o'clock, when the houses began to fall. Between this hour and one o'clock, P. M., ten or twelve tremendous shocks threw down the remainder of the brick buildings. By God's blessing, not one of the inhabitants was injured. But the earthquake shocks continuing, it was resolved that the settlement should be removed to the large island of Gillolo.

Gardiner entered the ruined town, and wandered in search of a house. The contrast between the overthrown abodes of men and the outskirts, was wonderful. The one was a ruin,—the other a perfect garden, whose wide lanes with long lines of bread fruit, bamboo, canary, (a large forest tree bearing almonds,) and mango, conducted him through cultivated grounds, interspersed with native houses, where Indian corn, sweet potatoes, and various kinds of tropical fruits were cultivated. A house, built of the branches and thatched with the leaves of the sago palm, was soon hired for a residence. Here, in the midst of a destruction which reminded them of a similar scene at Concepcion, the Gardiners thanked God for the merciful preservation which they had experienced. Had they been able to come direct, as they intended, from Copang to Ternate, they would have been in the town when it was destroyed.

When Gardiner delivered his letters of introduction to the Resident and the clergyman, and requested a pass to Sallawatty and Papua of the former, he was told that in the letter of which he was the bearer, information was given that he was suspected of being a political emissary of the

English government; and further, that a despatch had been forwarded to the Governor-General at Batavia, respecting him. A pass, therefore, could not be granted until an answer was received from the Governor-General.

This was a decisive stroke of policy which the upright and noble-hearted Gardiner could not understand. He wore no mask himself, and he never suspected that, under the smooth exterior of the Governor of Amboyna, whose dull eye told no tales, deep schemes were considered, and that the hand was sent out in advance to hold a friendly parley with a suspected man, and returned to write a note which was intended to arrest his steps, and destroy his hopes.

Had Captain Gardiner come without this note, the Resident of Ternate would have readily given him the required pass to Papua; but the reference to Batavia rendered this impossible. It so happened that the vessel which was to take the proposal of the inhabitants of Ternate to the Governor-General for removal, was still in the harbour. Gardiner therefore drew up a memorial, stating who he was, and giving his word as an English officer, a gentleman, and a Christian, that his sole object was to commence a Christian mission among the Papuans. The memorial concluded with a request for the desired pass.

As a three months' detention was now certain, Captain Gardiner began at once to study Malay, to improve Manoko in English, and to make the necessary preparations for proceeding, if the pass should be granted. But his constitution could not entirely throw off the fever with which he had been seized; therefore, after six weeks' residence at Ternate, during which time they experienced thirteen shocks of earthquake, they decided on going to Manado, on the island of Celebes, for change of air. It was time they did, for in case of illness little medical aid could be obtained here. Gardiner once sent a messenger for the doctor. The request being stated, the bearer of it was assured by the doctor's servant, that "his master was asleep and did not like to be disturbed."

As the Dutch allow no other metal but copper for the currency of these islands, the difficulty of procuring change for the little money required, was no less vexatious than amusing. Five pounds' worth of copper coins was a load for three men to carry. The rent of the palm-house was ten rupees a month. One hundred and twenty doits make a rupee; but as the current money consisted of doits and half-doits, ten rupees might consist of twenty-four hundred coins, and make a morning's work for landlord and tenant to count.

After a short trip of three days' travel, they reached Manado, close to which begins an ascent towards a high level, where are several villages, in one of which they fixed their residence. They travelled, according to the Celebes fashion, in three palanquins, with twelve men to each. Forty-four men brought up the baggage, thus making eighty in all.

The journey was completed in five hours: the rate of payment being to each bearer something less than a half-penny an English mile. Yet they were seemingly very happy, for they ran races with each other, and cheated the way with wild shouts and not unmusical songs. The village, where they were to find a temporary home, was about two thousand feet above the level of the sea. The floor of every house was elevated from six to eight or ten feet upon piles, so that Captain Gardiner very truly called it a "village on stilts." The houses were of wood, the roofs were thatched, a bamboo ladder served for a staircase, and the windows were square apertures with shutters. The governor's house, being empty, was lent by the Resident of Manado to the Gardiners. They remained here three months, waiting for the Governor-General's reply and found much pleasure in the society of Mr. and Mrs. Mattern, German missionaries who were deeply imbued with the spirit of their calling. The many displays of idolatrous folly which Gardiner witnessed here, gave him deep sorrow; but while such positive proofs of gross paganism were constantly being displayed, it is "still a cheering prospect," says he, "to think that, even in this place where Satan's seat is, there is also a servant of the Most High God."

He met with two other missionaries, Mr. Schwartz and Mr. Reidel, from whom he learned more of the complicated difficulties which stood in the way of Christian missions among the islanders of the South seas. Mr. Reidel, who had met with many difficulties in his missionary career, told him that, when he first entered on his duties at Tondano, he found many baptized persons, whose notions as to Christianity were confined to a few forms, such as the following:—It was their usual custom to dress themselves in black on Christmas day, that being the anniversary of Christ's death; and in white on New Year's day, that being the anniversary of his resurrection. When he tried to instruct them, he was told, "You need not call on me, I am a Christian," and after some questions, which only served to prove the ignorance of the persons who had been thus cheated into the profession of a religion, of which they comprehended nothing, Mr. Reidel said to one, "I will ask you one more question, 'Who is Jesus Christ?'" The reply was, "I do not know, unless he was the Resident of Manado."

This teaching was the result of a plan formed by the Dutch. They found the recruiting of native troops in these colonies a task of so much difficulty, that they were obliged to enlist soldiers from the heathen population of the Moluccas. This, however, did not please the people of Java, who, being Mohammedans, refused to serve in the same ranks with idolaters. An order, therefore, came from government, that proselytes were to be made to Christianity. Accordingly proselytes were made, and the greatest work was done in the neighbourhood of Manado. Alas! that Christian ministers could be found to baptize by government rule, so that the ranks of an army might be filled with recruits.

In the society of these true missionaries, who entered heartily into Gardiner's plans, three months passed pleasantly away; but at the end of that time a letter arrived from the Governor of Ternate, that despatches had been received from the Governor-General of Batavia, but not a word relative to Captain Gardiner. In this instance it was to be feared that "silence did not give consent." It was, however, of less consequence now. Although he had gained some encouraging information respecting the natives of Papua, the state of Gardiner's health was such that he felt it would be impossible for him to reside in the unhealthy climate of New Guinea for any length of time. But he was not the man to leave one stone unturned, in order to obtain the object of all his endeavours; for, had he received permission, his pioneering efforts might have smoothed the way for missionaries to follow. Leaving Toumahon for Manado, he had there an interview with the Governor of the Moluccas, in which, after parrying some very simple questions on the part of Captain Gardiner, one of which was, "Would missionaries be allowed to settle in Papua?" the governor declared that, considering the strong attachment of the Sultan to the Mohammedan faith, there was little ground to suppose that he would permit any other religion to be propagated in Papua, adding, "My impression undoubtedly is, that he would throw obstacles in your way."*

There was nothing to remain for now. A passage was at once taken to Ternate, where he found the Sultan of Tidore, an old man, nearly seventy. His dress was a red calico dressing gown, blue striped calico trowsers, and white turban. He said that for himself he was opposed to any attempt to teach Christianity in any part of his dominions; but that he should offer no opposition to any missionaries, who came with the consent of the Dutch government. The Papuans, he said, were a wrong-headed people, whom it would be impossible to convert. He had once himself acted as a missionary, and tried to convert the chief of Salawatty to the Mohammedan faith, but without success. He therefore shut the chief up in prison, and continued his endeavours to persuade him to adopt the true faith; but the chief was firm, and actually died in confinement, rather than accept the Sultan's terms.

Fully aware of all the difficulties which surrounded him, Gardiner, nevertheless, determined to go to Batavia, in order to have a personal interview with the governor. Accordingly, immediately on reaching his headquarters, he despatched a letter to that gentleman's secretary, requesting a reply to

*See Life of Gardiner, pp. 182—184.

the letter which he had written from Ternate. After more than a week had elapsed without receiving an answer, Gardiner went thirty miles into the country, in search of this uncommunicative governor. He first tried the government office; but the Governor-General had just gone home. Thither our indefatigable friend followed him, and was informed that he was at breakfast. "Present my card, if you please," said Gardiner, "I will wait in the verandah." After some time the servant re-appeared, and said he was sorry, but his honourable master was sick and could not be seen. Six days after this, a message was brought to Captain Gardiner, requesting his attendance at the Resident's office in Batavia. The Resident then addressed him as follows: "I am directed to inform you that none but 'burghers' are allowed to go to those places which you have requested permission to visit."

Suspicion and exclusion seemed to be the watchwords here; reminding one of the schoolboy, who sat apart from the rest, in solitary enjoyment of little islands of cake, and silenced all requests and stopped all longing looks, with the dignified announcement, "Those that ask, shan't have. Those that don't ask, don't want."

After receiving a similar reply, Captain Gardiner sailed with his family from Batavia, for the Cape of Good Hope. We cannot detain our readers by detailing the many events, such as the importing of slaves from Africa to serve as recruits for the army of Java, etc., and which caused the noble heart of Gardiner to throb with increased desire for the spread of the gospel in these benighted places; but choose rather to refer them to extracts from his journal.*

At the time when Gardiner took leave of Java, German missionaries were at Batavia, hoping to be allowed to proceed to Borneo. Recent events which have occurred there, have given hopes to Christian hearts, that from that central island will issue not only the strong hand which can put down the atrocities of Malay piracy, but the clear and distinct voice of missionary enterprise, which may tell to Malays, Papuans, and all island tribes, that Christ has died for all of them, and has sent them a message of peace.

* See Life of Gardiner, p. 189.

CHAPTER VIII.

CHILOE AND PATAGONIA.

Not to be wearied, not to be deterred.

UNSUCCESSFUL as Captain Gardiner had been in his attempt even to reach Papua, and injurious as the climate had proved to his health, he had never relaxed his efforts, until permission to proceed was refused. The voyage to Cape Town restored his health and that of his family, and he wrote—"With my renewed strength, I may say life, (for I consider it as given afresh,) I pray for grace to be enabled to devote it to the service of Him who redeemeth my life from destruction, and crowneth me with mercy and loving-kindness."

Captain Gardiner had now determined to make another attempt to communicate with the Indians of South America. Passing near the coast of Port Natal, he almost caught a glimpse of the distant hills, where the little settlement of Hambanati had once excited so much hope. He reached Cape Town on November 4th, and sailing from thence to Rio Janeiro, and doubling Cape Horn, landed at Valparaiso, on March 10th, 1841, and in less than a fortnight was ready for his exploring journey. It will be remembered that his efforts in 1838–9, were made from Concepcion and Valdivia, but failed because the chiefs were either in the receipt of Chilian pay, or defying the Chilian government. Still, in a country of so vast an extent, where there were so many tribes, he began to indulge a hope of success in some yet untried quarter. He had recourse to books, and he found an account of some independent tribes of Pehuenches, dwelling in the remote valleys of the Cordillera, who were, from their secluded position, alike shut out from war, from Romish influence, and from Chilian commissaries; he hoped, from what he had heard of their friendly disposition, he should be able to open a mission.

His first attempt to reach this tribe, was by the Planchon Pass, between Talca and San Fernando. He travelled on horseback, with an attendant, a mule carrying such baggage as was necessary. But after a most fatiguing journey he found it impossible to get either guide or interpreter, and the whole way among the Cordilleras so crowded with difficulties, that he retraced his steps to Valparaiso, and prepared for a voyage to the island of Chiloe.

The interval between his return and the obtaining of a passage, was spent in an endeavour to promote the circulation of the Bible among the Spanish Americans. A large case of Bibles and tracts, which had arrived from England in his absence, was at this time bonded in Captain Gardiner's name, in the custom-house at Valparaiso. As they could not be taken out without permission from government, a formal request was now made to the authorities at Santiago, for leave to enter a case of "Bibles and other religious books," on payment of the usual dues. To the surprise of most, and joy of Gardiner, a simple affirmative was received. This proof of liberality encouraged him to hope that if he could once gain permission from the Indians to settle among them, no opposition would be made by the Chilian government.

In ten days after leaving Valparaiso, the Gardiners arrived at the beautiful harbour of San Carlos, in the island of Chiloe. One of their fellow-passengers proved to be the identical Friar Manuel, who had poisoned the mind of Neggiman, the chief, against Gardiner, and influenced his refusal of the plan of residing among his people. The hostile feeling of this evil genius, however, was not suspected; nevertheless its venom was soon felt.

The friar, on landing, lost no time in spreading reports injurious to his late fellow-passenger. He told them to be on their guard, for Gardiner was not what he seemed to be, but a most dangerous man, and had come for the purpose of disturbing their religious faith, and making proselytes to his own perverted creed. This was enough for the gossips of San Carlos; it was soon rumoured that the foreign padre was an heretical bishop in disguise.

There were two ways of proceeding to the passage of the Cordillera; one by Osorno, where the road was so bad that it was hardly safe to ride; and the other in a more direct line, and only one-fourth of the distance, but without any road at all. However, as Osorno was in Friar Manuel's route, and he would not have exerted a friendly influence on those among whom Gardiner travelled, the shorter way was resolved upon. For the first few miles it would be necessary to cut through the wood with axes, and he endeavoured to hire a party of men to accompany and assist him. A North American sailor offered his services, and he was commissioned to hire others; nothing, however, would induce the Chilians to help a man on whom rested the ban of the church, so the expedition had to be given up.

The friar finding his purpose accomplished, seemed at length to think that he had gone too far. Before he left San Carlos, he came to Captain Gardiner, and adopting a familiar tone, said, "Let us be friends, man. You wanted a Chilidugu dictionary, and here is one." So saying, he produced a dictionary from under his poncho, which had in vain been sought for in the libraries and monasteries, and was now thankfully received.

As the strange reports which had been circulated about the Englishman on his first arrival died away, they were succeeded by others equally unfounded.

But whilst those whom he came to serve, incapable of appreciating his motives, were endeavouring to thwart his benevolent purposes, he was quietly pursuing his usual course. If his plan failed for approaching the uncivilized Indians, he fell back upon another important object, that of circulating the Scriptures among the Romanists. Having taken a house at San Carlos for six months, he now exerted himself successfully in circulating Bibles and tracts in Chiloe.

However unwilling to do so, Gardiner was obliged to give up his project of civilizing the South American Indians, for where could any other attempt be made to communicate with them? Like the Arabs, the Indian tribes roaming between the Cordillera and the Atlantic were wild and free; their hand was against every man, and every man's hand was against them. Through this scene of devastation Gardiner had at first passed. But when he turned more hopefully to districts where the white and red men were at peace, the dark Papal shadow clouded all there with gloom.

Obliged therefore to abandon all hopes of reaching the Indian population, where they are most civilized and least migratory, his thoughts turned towards the south. The Patagonians, (of whom we have already given a description,) about Gregory Bay, had always evinced a friendly disposition to foreigners; and believing that the Falkland Islands, now under the protection of the British flag, might become the key to the aborigines, both of Patagonia and Terra del Fuego, he made immediate preparations for going there. To obtain a passage to the Falklands, the Gardiners returned to Valparaiso, where they were at once met by their friend Mr. Armstrong, and accepted his invitation to remain during their stay at his house. Leaving his family thus hospitably entertained, Captain Gardiner went to Santiago and Quillota with a large package of Bibles, some of which he sold, some he gave away, and the rest he consigned to a bookseller in Santiago, who undertook to promote their sale, although they had not the orthodox notes appended to them.

After remaining a month at Valparaiso, Captain Gardiner embarked with his family for the Falkland Islands, which they reached in safety, although, twice during the passage, they were exposed to serious danger.

As they advanced to the southward, and the sun shone brightly, they obtained so clear a view of Terra del Fuego, that they were not only able to gain a general idea of its bold and rugged outline, but to trace several of the points mentioned in the survey of Captains King and Fitzroy. They rounded the Cape without a storm, and passed near to Staten Island, afterwards a point of so much interest to Captain Gardiner, and anchored in Berkeley Sound, just in time to spend Christmas-day at Port Louis.

Though this was midsummer, the island had a

dreary aspect from the absence of trees and all cultivation. The country was undulating, and covered with short grass and a sort of heather. The settlement consisted of a few cottages, one of which was lent to the Gardiners for a week, the usual occupants being absent on a hunting expedition. In the meantime they were kindly assisted by some English sailors to erect the little wooden cottage that had been brought from Valparaiso.

Captain Gardiner was disappointed in his expectation of finding frequent communication between these islands and the Strait of Magellan. The government, in re-asserting the right of England to the Falklands, had warned off the ships of other nations from the sealing ground. American whalers and sealers, therefore, went only to the uninhabited islands for water and wild game, thereby avoiding harbour dues. It was, therefore, no easy matter to obtain a passage to the straits. Many applications were made to captains of vessels who entered the harbour, but one had not provisions enough to lengthen his voyage, and another would not risk his vessel in these narrow and dangerous seas.

In this dilemma Gardiner was obliged to engage a passage in a crazy old schooner called the *Montgomery*, which, with ragged sails, and with sheathing torn off, was only capable of running from harbour to harbour among the islands. The westernmost of these, called New Island, being more frequented by sealers and whalers, was considered a kind of post-office, and leaving his family at Port Louis, Gardiner went there, taking with him a servant, a tent, and a store of provisions, intending to live in Robinson Crusoe fashion, till he could get a passage to the Strait of Magellan.

They anchored in Ship Harbour, New Island, on the 11th of March, 1842, where they found two whalers busily engaged in fishing. The captains were very civil and friendly, but could not be induced to leave the fishing-ground for a long time. It was now the height of the season; seals were in plenty, and they had taken three whales within a month.

Learning that a whale might be worth, on the average, one thousand dollars, or two hundred pounds, Gardiner offered that sum, if either of the vessels would run across with him to Patagonia. The reply was, that at any other time they would gladly give him a passage for nothing, that if their visitor pleased, he should be welcome to stay on board either of their vessels till another opportunity offered of proceeding farther; but while fish were so plentiful, they could not move.

Mr. Back, the master of the *Somerset*, had lately been in the straits, and stated that he had fallen in with a tribe of Patagonians, among whom was a Creole Spaniard named San Leon, who had acquired great influence over the natives. The Patagonians are very much under the sway of pretended wizards. San Leon, a man of reckless courage, being subjected to the incantations of one of these wizards, defied, and shot him with a pistol in the presence of his tribe. The spectators were horror-struck, but transferred their fear of the wizard to San Leon himself; who, by this desperate act, gained for himself almost the authority of a chief. After this, he assumed a right over a large district, about Possession Bay, which he called his hunting-ground, and undertook to supply guanaco meat to vessels anchoring near the narrows.

This news made Gardiner more desirous than ever to proceed. The master of the *Montgomery* had heard with wondering satisfaction of the liberal offer made to the captains of the whalers, and he now proposed to perform the required voyage for two hundred pounds, having first rendered his crazy schooner as seaworthy as possible, by caulking her, and borrowing a sail. Having no alternative, Gardiner, rather than wait an unlimited time, agreed to sail in the vessel, but positively refused to give more than half the sum demanded.

Before the necessary preparations for the voyage could be made, the intervention of the Sunday gave him an opportunity of recalling to the minds of those around him, the long-forgotten duty of the Sabbath. He proposed to have service on board the *Montgomery*, but only two men could be found, the rest were all absent or intoxicated. Alas! that there should be such general neglect of the Sabbath, which is God's everlasting gift to man, among soldiers and sailors. There is a rough frankness about the British or American sailor, and a liberal kind-heartedness, but the continual temptation to indulge in dram-drinking, has the effect of diverting his better qualities into a wrong direction. The preparations for fitting out the *Montgomery* for sea were soon made; the sail was borrowed, and the poor little schooner stood out to sea in its old age, presenting its worn-out sides to the broad waves, and struggled along for the Patagonian coast. It entered the Strait of Magellan on the fifth day after sailing, and drifted near the shore of Terra del Fuego. Guanacos were seen, but no Fuegians.

On the following day, a smoke was observed, which induced Captain Gardiner to land with his men, and make a fire to attract the natives. After a short time the islanders began to approach, shouting as they advanced, but, pausing at some distance, they also kindled a fire. Supposing this to be an invitation to join them, but not wishing to have the interview at a distance from the boat, Gardiner made a signal that the invitation had come from him, by putting more fuel on his fire and retaining his position. Seeming to understand this, two of the Fuegians descended towards the beach. Gardiner met them, holding a coloured handkerchief and some red worsted tape. Both these men were clothed in guanaco-skin cloaks with the hair outside. They were about five feet ten inches in height, with broad shoulders and chests, but their legs were lean and out of proportion to their solid frames. Each had a bow and quiver of arrows. They spoke loudly and made very plain signs for their visitors to go away. They received the presents offered them, such as brass buttons, a clasp knife, and a worsted comforter, and condescended to sit down; but their manner was sullen and repulsive. Gardiner made several attempts to overcome this determined reserve. A small looking-glass was handed to the elder Fuegian, who received it, and was grimly stowing it under his cloak, when Gardiner held it up to his face and that of his companion. They laughed sourly when they saw the representation of their smeared visages. A clasp-knife was next offered; they turned it over as if expecting something pictorial was also there. The knife was opened, they expressed as much pleasure as was consistent with the thick paint on their faces, but no friendly sign was returned. A few Spanish words and sentences were then tried, but in vain. Gardiner had picked up a few Patagonian words; these he now uttered with great care, but there was no response. Johnson was then directed to go towards the boat; this action seemed to give the first unmingled satisfaction to the Fuegians, who lost no time in making signs for Gardiner to follow him. As there was nothing else to be done, he shook hands with them twice, and having induced them to exchange an arrow for a handkerchief, took his leave.

The schooner passing through the Strait on the next day entered Gregory Bay. Having landed, Captain Gardiner and Johnson endeavoured to find the Patagonian encampment, of which the whaling captain had spoken. A walk of eight miles brought them to an old encampment. The grass was beaten down, nine hollow places showed where fires had been lately burning, and traces of many footsteps still remained. Close by was a spring of water, which widened into a small brook; and the ground in various places was quite red with a profusion of berries, similar to cranberries. They also observed thorny bushes ten feet high, and patches of wild celery and clover. Having ascended the Gregory heights, they observed two wreaths of smoke in the direction of Oazy Harbour, to which place they went in the schooner on the same afternoon, and anchored opposite the Indian fires.

On the following morning some of the natives came on board. After these men had been entertained, the camp was visited. Many of the tents were of horse-hide, semicircular in shape, and entirely open. They were filled with men, women, and children. Lean horses and dogs were to be seen here and there. In a conversation held in Spanish with San Leon, who sat among a crowd of Patagonians, he stated that he had been with the tribe twelve years, and that "old Maria," who is frequently spoken of in the published voyages of Capt. Fitzroy, was dead. He also said, when he understood the errand of Captain Gardiner, that American missionaries had come to Patagonia, but could not stay, because the Fuegians were such thieves that they not only ate up their provisions, but cut up their books. Captain Gardiner, being informed that many of the people had for a long time been absent, but daily were expected to return, resolved to wait for their arrival. No opposition being made to his remaining, the canvas tent, which had been brought from the Falklands, was set up. It was of a gable shape, and closed at each end with bullock-hides, except where a small opening served as a door.

On the first night the inhabitants of this tent were disturbed by the dogs, which endeavoured to make a meal of the hides that filled the end of the tent. In the morning, a fresh coat of tar was put on the canvas, and thus the dogs were put off the scent. On the second evening, when the two inmates had composed themselves to rest, they were startled by the entrance of a long Patagonian, who, saying "I go sleep," very leisurely coiled himself up for that purpose. Johnson expostulated in elaborate English without effect, but Gardiner, touching the Patagonian with one hand, and distinctly repeating the word "Go," the intruder departed.

The tent with its tarred canvas and hides, as well as its owners, was an object of much curiosity. The natives moved their tents, and pitched them exactly behind that of their visitors, in a row of seventeen. The women came first mounted on horses, a load of poles being on one side, a store of meat on the other, and a pile of skins in the centre, which formed a seat for the rider. Then came the men, and a village was built in two or three hours.

Gardiner had expected that they would crowd round the novel tent and try to effect an entrance, but they were not riotous, and upon the whole behaved well.

But now alarming news came from the schooner, of a misunderstanding between the natives and the crew. Gardiner instantly procured a horse with the payment of some tobacco, and rode down to the Point, from whence he went on board the schooner. It turned out that the master of the vessel had requested San Leon to provide him with some meat for the crew. This he had agreed to do, and told certain natives to "seek guanaco." They went, disappeared behind the hills for some time, and then returned without any thing. The boat of the schooner came for the promised meat; but no sooner had it touched the beach than a party of natives came down, seized the painter, and said that no one should go back to the ship till they had been paid for their trouble in "seeking guanaco." San Leon, who was on board the schooner, called out to the boat's crew not to land, and on hearing this, they cut the rope and returned on board.

This adventure proved San Leon's authority to be very small; but he explained the matter by declaring that the offenders were not Patagonians, but

Fuegians. This afterwards proved correct; and the Patagonians, angry at these libellers of their race, were with difficulty prevented from entering into a quarrel with them.

San Leon now declared his wish to go in the schooner to Port Famine. Gardiner reminded him of the thievish and reckless conduct of the Fuegians, but San Leon assured him that nothing need be feared, as the Patagonians intended to remain where they were till his return. The *Montgomery* then proceeded to Port Famine with San Leon for a load of wood, and Captain Gardiner and Johnson remained with the Patagonians.

In the absence of their chief, but little communication could be held. A few monosyllabic requests, replies, and directions were interchanged, but nothing serious occurred to lead to any rupture. They were very curious and observant, but by no means troublesome. So friendly did they appear, that Johnson imagined he could safely leave the camp kettle boiling on the fire, while he took a walk. But the temptation was too great. Venturing into the tent, they peeped into the kettle, and abstracted the contents—good ship's biscuit. The nights were very cold, and the wind entered under the covering of the tent; therefore it was necessary to erect a wall of sods around it.

The country is broken by low hills, between which are narrow brooks, ponds, and lagoons. Grass, clover, and celery grow there, and in some places the ground is carpeted with a creeping, heathy plant, the berries of which are gathered and eaten by the young Patagonians.

On the return of the schooner, Captain Gardiner rode down to the coast to see San Leon. While he was absent another body of Patagonians arrived. The chief, Wissale, was a man of powerful frame, and as he stood with his guanaco-skin cloak muffled round him, he appeared of gigantic proportions, though in reality not more than six feet high. He received Captain Gardiner in a friendly manner, and told him that he and his party had been absent eight months, and had purchased one hundred and twenty horses. He was accompanied by a North American black, named Isaac, who spoke English, and proved a far better interpreter than San Leon. He had woolly hair, and was dressed in a skin cloak like the Patagonians. He said that about three years before he had deserted from a whaler at the Rio Gallegas, and had ever since been with Wissale's people.

Presents, consisting of brass buttons, knives, handkerchiefs, tobacco, and biscuit, were distributed among the chief and his family, after which Wissale and Isaac visited the stranger's tent. After some friendly civilities, Gardiner told his errand, which no doubt the chief clearly understood through Isaac. He replied, "It was well; they should be brothers." Being reminded of the thievish propensities of the Northern Fuegians, the Yacanas, who were always visiting his tribe, he answered, "He himself would protect his friend. He would tell his own people to take care of his friend's property. Nothing should be stolen."

When it was explained to him that the only reason which induced his friend to wish to live with the Patagonians, was in order to teach them good things out of the book he saw before him, he replied, "That he should like to be taught those good things, and he would teach Captain Gardiner his language."

After this very satisfactory conversation, tea was prepared, which Wissale seemed to like. He remained for some time after tea, and sat in silence while Gardiner read from his Bible, explained the passage, and offered prayer and thanksgiving.

On Sunday, service was held in the tent; three men from the schooner, and Isaac attended. On Monday, a consultation was evidently held respecting the white visitor, above whose tent rose the protecting spear of Wissale; an old patriarch being listened to with great attention. Isaac explained that the old man knew one very short way to the hearts of his hearers. Pointing to the tobacco and him who gave it, with high approval, he said that, "The stranger was good and friendly to them, and it would be good for them to treat him well, for if they did so, he would give them plenty of tobacco." A murmur of approbation followed this speech.

All things thus promising well, Gardiner determined on bringing his family from the Falklands, to reside among them for a time. The schooner was in want of meat, and Wissale gave the order to "hunt guanaco." A large party rode out on horseback accompanied by the hungry dogs, and afterwards, on coming near the hunting-ground, separated in order to encircle a considerable range. Here and there an ostrich started up from the grass, and dashed away, followed by some of the dogs. One ostrich only was pulled down, and several guanacos.

Gardiner requested San Leon to take charge of his tent, &c., and taking a friendly leave of Wissale, embarked with Johnson on his return voyage.

They made a quick passage to New Island, where they found the whalers still chasing the "monsters of the deep;" but the voyage to Port Louis, in which they encountered a heavy gale, was both tedious and unsafe. Gardiner found some English vessels in the harbour, but his ardent wish that one among them might be found to take him to Patagonia, was doomed to disappointment. He was, therefore, obliged to wait for six months, as no vessel was found able or willing to aid him, and he would not risk his family in the crazy *Montgomery*.

In the mean time, one of them sailing to Rio Janeiro, our missionary pioneer sent a letter to the Secretary of the Church Missionary Society there, and after detailing the good dispositions of Wissale and his people, requested that an ordained missionary might be sent to Patagonia, and stated his intention of remaining there with his family until a mission should be established.

There was no stated chaplain at this time in the colony; the governor read the Church service at the government-house every Sunday morning; and Gardiner, wishing to do something for the sailors, and others who did not trouble themselves to go up thither, conducted worship in the evening at the house of one of the settlers, for a few weeks. But, although several persons attended at first, their numbers gradually decreased, and the service was at length given up.

The presence of the two English ships, *Erebus* and *Terror*, in the harbour for a whole winter, was an event in the history of East Falkland. For a time it more than doubled the population of the island; and the friendliness of their captains was an especial benefit to our travellers.

These gentlemen approved of Gardiner's prospective missionary schemes, and also showed a lively interest in New Zealand, and the progress of Christianity there.

On September 8th, the discovery ships sailed for Cape Horn, and in the following month two schooners, the *Sociedad* and the *Princess Royal*, anchored in the sound. Gardiner found that, for a good sum, the latter would have been put at his disposal, but intelligence received by the *Philomel* altered all his plans.

It had never been Gardiner's plan to locate himself as a missionary, but simply to prepare the way for one, and if he found an opening, to hold the ground till a clergyman and his coadjutors should be sent out, to carry on the work more effectually than he could do.

He now learned that the Society to which he looked for support, was under the necessity of reducing its expenditure, on account of a temporary falling off in its funds; and that, consequently, there was no prospect of aid from that quarter, at least for a long time. He, therefore, determined to go at once to England, and personally plead the claims of Patagonia, but before sailing he was happy to be assured that Captain Sulivan of H. M. S. *Philomel*, would lend his support, if a mission were established in Patagonia.

He sailed on October 28th, for Rio Janeiro, where he remained until December. On the 12th, a whaler came into the harbour, and Gardiner going on board, heard news from Gregory Bay. The hut and its contents were still untouched, San Leon taking charge of it. Isaac, too, was there, and professed an intention of remaining with the Patagonians. The following day, the Gardiners sailed in a Swedish ship for England, and landed at St. Ives, on February 17th, 1843, after an absence of six years.

CHAPTER IX.

THE BIBLE IN SOUTH AMERICA.

"Still go on, and to the pole
Heavenly bounties safely bear;
Till the Gospel-heralds tell
All the Gospel-message there;
And the darkened savage find
Jesus, Saviour of mankind."

WE have now come to a new era in Gardiner's life. Hitherto, with a grand object before him, the pursuit of which occupied his energies and employed his thoughts, he had the solace of domestic life in his disappointments and difficulties. It was now time that the education of his children should be attended to, with more method than was possible when their home was so uncertain. Henceforth his journeys were to be taken alone.

His first effort, on reaching England, was to press on the attention of the Church Missionary Society, the propriety of founding a mission in Patagonia. But their financial difficulties obliged them to turn a deaf ear to this proposal, as they had been forced to do on similar appeals for enlarging and extending their missions in India and Africa.

The same ill-success was experienced on application to the Wesleyan and London Missionary Societies.* He also printed an earnest appeal, hoping that some of his fellow-Christians might come forward to aid him in forming a society for the special benefit of South America. A few extracts are given:—

"By the good providence of God I have lately returned from South America, where, after endeavouring for more than three years to prepare the way for the entrance of a missionary among the native tribes of the southern section of that continent, it has pleased the Lord at length to vouchsafe as much success as I could have anticipated. The Patagonians are willing to be instructed; my tent and my baggage remain among them; and, but for the accounts which were received of the reductions, which it had become necessary for the Church Missionary Society to make in many of their stations, and the impossibility, under existing circumstances, of their being able to undertaking any new mission, I should at this present moment have been residing with my family among them.

"These tidings, which were received only a few months ago, occasioned our immediate return, not being able alone at our own cost, and having no

* See extract from one of his letters, p. 228.

authorized missionary with us, to occupy the ground. . . .

"Let us remember Him who, though he was rich, yet for our sakes became poor; who willeth that all men should be saved and come to the knowledge of the truth; and who will not be satisfied, until he has received the fulness of that harvest, which the travail of his soul is still ripening; until many, from the East and from the *West*, from out of all kindreds, and nations, and tongues, shall be gathered into his fold, and sit down with Abraham, and Isaac, and Jacob, in the kingdom of his Father.

"That the God of all grace and truth, who can bring strength out of weakness, and can make the feeblest instruments subservient to his glory, may vouchsafe his blessing upon this humble endeavour in his name, is the sincere prayer of

"Your faithful and sincere friend,

"ALLEN F. GARDINER.

"*March* 13*th*, 1843."

There was little response to this appeal; for the disasters which had overtaken the Zulu Mission had tended greatly to cool the enthusiasm of those who had been warm in the cause. South America, too, did not come within the range of their sympathy, as did Africa and India; but believing it to be the "natural inheritance of pope and pagan," seemed disposed to leave it to its fate.

Gardiner, however, who did not understand hesitation, was not to be turned from his great purpose, even when meeting with such a cold response from his friends. He believed that a good prospect was now opening for a mission in Patagonia, and he was determined to employ the pause now forced upon him, in circulating the word of God among the Spanish-speaking inhabitants of South America; and any success which he might meet with in the attempt, must prove to the friends of missions at home, that earlier efforts might have resulted in earlier success. From the time when the Chilian government had allowed a case of Bibles to pass through the custom-house of Valparaiso, he felt that a great opening existed for their circulation throughout the South American republics; for, if admitted in Chili, it was not likely they would be rejected elsewhere. He now resolved to try whether the government permission would be negatived by the local influence of the priests.

In his contemplated enterprise, he never lost sight of the effect which any success he might meet with must have on his great object, namely, a mission to Patagonia, as a key to the heathens of South America. Having obtained a grant of Bibles, Testaments, books, and tracts, he once more sailed toward the southern continent, resolved to prove whether or not it was possible to circulate the Scriptures in the interior provinces, in the very heart of the country, among the Spanish population.

Seven days after sailing from Falmouth, the packet reached Madeira, where they remained two days. This gave Captain Gardiner an opportunity of visiting Dr. Kalley, a Scotch missionary whom he found in prison. His only crime was circulating tracts and Bibles, which brought upon himself the fierce indignation of the authorities. Still he went on, quietly and steadily, and succeeded in setting on foot several schools, in which no other books than the Bible and the spelling book were used. In order to stop these proceedings, Dr. Kalley was imprisoned, and some of his schools were closed.

Gardiner found him in a comfortable room, provided for him by a friend; his wife and mother were with him. They had a very earnest conversation together, on the subject which was in the heart of both, and on taking his leave, our missionary pioneer felt encouraged rather than depressed, in his present purpose, from witnessing the all-sustaining effect of divine grace on the happy family he was just leaving in prison.

Three weeks after leaving Madeira, the vessel made the port of Pernambuco, and Gardiner finding a Sardinian schooner bound to the river Plate, he made arrangements for his books to be forwarded to Buenos Ayres, and after finding some difficulty in gaining a passage, sailed for Monte Video. In consequence of news brought by a coasting vessel, there was some doubt entertained of the possibility of proceeding to Monte Video, as General Rosas had blockaded the harbour. While the rest were occupied in discussing the probable settlement of this quarrel, Captain Gardiner retired to his cabin for solemn prayer, that he might be guided and protected by wisdom and power from above, on the difficult mission now before him.

From an officer who came on board from a boat belonging to the man-of-war brig *Republicana*, they learned that, although a close blockade was kept up by the Buenos Ayres squadron, no impediment would now be offered to the further progress of the schooner. They accordingly reached Monte Video harbour in safety, but hearing that another schooner was to sail the same evening for Buenos Ayres, Gardiner determined to proceed, and conveyed his baggage on board before landing.

On the following morning the schooner arrived at Buenos Ayres. It happened to be a feast day, and no sooner was Gardiner's baggage landed on the beach, than the officer of the custom-house, after grumbling at their being brought to him on a feast day, ordered them to be placed in durance till the custom-house should be opened on the following morning. So all boxes were carried off, and there was nothing left for Gardiner, but to yield to what could not be helped.

As he had arrived before his books, he employed the interval in preparing a wagon for his journey, and getting certain tracts which he had arranged on the voyage, translated into Spanish.

In answer to an inquiry about the sale of Spanish Bibles, an English bookseller stated that he had been supplied with some, but they would not sell, being the wrong sort; that is, they had blue edges instead of red. Blue was the colour adopted by the Monte Videans in the war, therefore blue edges disqualified a Bible from being of use to a Buenos Ayrean!

On the 11th of November, his wagon with the required number of horses and peones, entered the wide plains of the Pampas. As they advanced, the clover with its varied flowers ornamented the plains; but the most remarkable sight was the large waving tract of thistles, which were often seven feet high. The post-houses on the road afforded tolerable accommodation for the night to one who was not very fastidious. Here and there rumours were heard of the Indians, who, taking advantage of the war among the white population, had made nine predatory expeditions during the last six months, carrying off women and children, and driving away cattle. These ominous reports were, however, balanced by a little local knowledge. The thistles, which are so annoying to the postilions, are, as soon as they reach their full growth, a protection to travellers from the incursions of bare-legged Indians. The thistle district extended to the limits of the Buenos Ayrean province.

They now entered the province of Santa Fe. The thistles were at first higher than the top of a man's head on horseback; but as the road became clear of thistles, it deepened in mud, and the rumours of Indian attacks became more threatening.

Nothing could induce Captain Gardiner to travel on Sunday. Even in this dangerous part of the road he kept to his determination, though it was impossible to ascertain whether the reports were false or true. He had planned to rest for the Sunday at the post-house of Esquina de la Guardia, but news arriving of an expected attack on that very post-house, he waited for further intelligence, and spent the Sunday where he then was. On Monday morning it was ascertained that the story of the Indians was a false alarm. A party of gauchos, or Spaniards of the Pampas, had been mistaken for them.

On entering the province of Cordova, there was little further danger from the Indians, who are kept in perpetual check by the Cordovese government. They had now been twelve days on their journey, when the Cordova hills were seen in the distance, at first appearing but little elevated above the plain, but the very glimpse of a rising ground was charming, after a long, dreary, desolate journey on an almost level ground for five hundred miles.

A river separated them from what may be called the tangled and thorny district. The shrubs and mimosa trees were delightful to look at, but not so pleasant to pass through. The peones protect themselves with a piece of hide, slung over the horse's neck before the saddle, and strapped underneath.

In every village is a rude mill for grinding corn, standing in an open place at the entrance, quite unprotected, and evidently public property. Before reaching the city of Cordova they were stopped by a river, which it was impossible to cross without additional help. Being obliged to remain here over night, Gardiner made a pleasant acquaintance with an English medical man, Dr. Gordon, who gave him much useful information. He resided in Cordova, and in the morning rode on homewards, requesting Gardiner to call upon him as soon as he reached the city.

At three o'clock in the afternoon of the 24th of November, the wagon, with four mounted peones, entered the deserted streets; it was the hour of siesta—every one was enjoying sweet sleep. The officer of the customs had retired for a nap, so the traveller had nothing to do but pace the silent street, and wonder what would be the effect of a universal siesta if introduced into England.

Not a shop was open. But while Gardiner was thus wandering round, an elderly lady, whose curiosity had overcome her desire for slumber, appeared at the door of a house and invited him to enter and rest himself, only asking him, by way of recompense, that he would tell her whence he came, whither he was going, and what his business was. Before these queries could be satisfactorily answered, the custom-house officer appeared, and speedily inspecting the baggage, suffered the cases of books to pass without examination. Captain Gardiner then proceeded to call on others, but the answer was ever, "*dormiendo.*"

In the evening, Gardiner had an interview with Dr. Gordon and the Governor. When the object of the present journey was explained, the latter became very reserved, but offered no opposition; and in answer to his request gave him two letters, to the governors of Estero and Tucuman.

Leaving Cordova on the next morning, he was requested at the first post-house, to take the letter-bags in his wagon, so that the letter-carrier might act as postilion. He did so for one stage, but declined any further service, not liking the responsibility of a South American postman, so the packages were tied up in an old poncho, swung across a horse's back, and the whole entrusted to the guidance of a lad.

The detention at Cordova was fortunate for Gardiner, as, had he stopped at a certain post-house, no human power could have saved him from certain robbery, and possible murder. As it was, the wagon passed safely by. The province of Cordova abounds in thorny mimosa, and a variety of palm-trees, one of which has large fan-like leaves, with every point armed with a sharp spike, and each leaf divided almost to the stem.

When the horses are turned loose in the evening, it is necessary, in a country so covered with bushes, to have a bell slung round the neck of one of them, and even then they are often difficult to catch. Gardiner, as they entered the province of Santiago, found the road very bad; in one part it was necessary to hire twenty horses, to drag the wagon through swamps and quagmires.

The post-masters were, here and there, willing to receive tracts. At the post-house of Juanilla, the conductor of a troop of caravans saw Gardiner giving a few tracts to the post-master, and asked for some for himself, promising to circulate them.

After an eight days' journey, Santiago was reached, where Gardiner, being provided with letters of introduction from Dr. Gordon, was received with much hospitality. Great curiosity to see the Bibles was exhibited. One box was opened, but the visitors were determined to see the contents of another box. They handed the books about, examining the binding, paper, and type, but showed no signs of quitting the room until eleven o'clock at night, when a second box was opened and an arrangement made for a regular sale next day.

Soon after breakfast, some ladies came to purchase books; several friars wanted novels and medical books, but no Bibles. The room was soon filled with purchasers, but as they handed books about to each other, and so intermixed volumes, there was so much confusion that it was impossible to keep an exact account of the books sold. Nevertheless, it was gratifying to find such a demand. A gentleman came forward and offered to help in the task of selling the books, and when this laborious day was over, the two salesmen determined to make better arrangements, if possible, for the next day. Don Jose provided two tables as a sort of counter, and Captain Gardiner began at daylight arranging all his books on the tables for sale; all the time, however, loud knockings at the door were heard, and many inquiries were made, as to when the sale would commence.

When all was ready, he went out, locking the door behind him, and proceeded on an errand which few other persons would have delayed so long. Before leaving England, he had caught a severe cold, which ended in ulceration of the throat. The inflammation, which was not subdued on the voyage, was increased on the journey from Buenos Ayres to Cordova, but his eagerness to proceed was so great, that he gave it no attention there. But now, the heat of the previous day's sale, and the necessity of so much talking, increased the pain and inflammation, and he felt himself obliged to consult a physician, who advised him to trifle with it no longer, and ordered a blister. Gardiner having made up his mind to do so, when he reached Tucuman, that is, in four or five days' time after another severe journey, went back to his room for another day's sale of books.

The place was crowded and the sale rapid; nevertheless, in the course of the day, it was whispered about that the foreigner was not a good Catholic, and a silver crucifix was thereupon handed round to be kissed. It was presented to him, but his refusal produced no demonstration—the sale went on. The governor sent for a tract by name, and a lady, whose character for kindness and charity stood very high, assisted in the sale, taking the place of Don José when he was obliged to be absent. Many pleasant incidents occurred, which, to relate, we fear would tire our readers, but served greatly to encourage Gardiner, who, after remaining at Santiago five days, commenced his journey to Tucuman.

The Sunday was spent in a post-house, but not in quiet; the post-master annoyed him with his company. The journey, although most unpleasant, was, happily, a short one; the sand flew in clouds, as in an African desert, and the dust was so great, that often the two nearest postilions were not to be seen; all threatening serious results to a traveller with a severely inflamed throat. The sun struck with such force through the canvas covering, that the wagon became heated like an oven. The little grass that appeared was dry and parched. The first sight of Tucuman was pleasant indeed, for here he might rest.

The governor received Captain Gardiner with great civility. It was soon rumoured throughout the town, that large cases of books were to be sold on the following day. Before retiring to rest, Gardiner applied the blister, which the French physician at Santiago had ordered, and before the sale commenced, he had a little experience of the Tucuman method of curing a sore throat. His landlady offered to dress the blister, which she did, by first spreading an ointment on two vine-leaves, and then taking off the blister. This she accomplished with great rapidity, taking off the skin also, and then laid the vine-leaves on the bare flesh, producing intense agony; at which the operator was, by no means, surprised, although she seemed much astonished to hear that this flaying-alive system was not practised in England.

When the hour for the sale arrived, the door was crowded, first with peeping children, and afterwards with others, and it was a hard task to preserve order. Many books and tracts, with a few Bibles, were sold, when Captain Gardiner was able to make an arrangement with a bookseller to take all the books, together with a number of Bibles and Testaments. Being now at the end of his journey, and having met with greater success than he could have hoped for in the sale of Bibles, he thought it would be well to send to one or more of the padres a present of a Spanish Bible. This he did, and to two of them who were well spoken of, a parcel of Bibles was sent, also two hundred Testaments were put in the hands of Don Manuel, the bookseller, who was very particular in inquiring if there was any additions to the Scriptures in the shape of notes, etc.

Gardiner gave notice that he wished to be left in quiet on the next day, which was Sunday, but it proved a day of interruption and anxiety.

About half-past nine an officer of police entered, and announced that the Curé had given out in his sermon, that the stranger, who had just come among them with books for sale, was a heretic, and that the books were not proper to be read. The officer, in consequence of this statement, demanded that a copy of each book should be sent to the police office for inspection. Gardiner informed him that the books were at Don Manuel's, and defended his books warmly, at the same time urging, "That similar books had been sold in Santiago without hindrance." "Perhaps so," said the officer, "but the Curé would object."

After some further conversation, in which Gardiner asked him if he thought "the Bible, God's own revelation, an heretical book?" he answered, "No, not the correct word of God." "Well, the Bibles I have brought are the true word of God, without notes, or additions of any kind." "Still," said the officer, "there is a difficulty. *I myself think the books are good, but the people are very ignorant.*" After some further discourse the officer took leave, and from his whole manner, which was civil and almost friendly, Gardiner felt that, although it might be necessary to inspect the books, he had no hostile influence to dread from the public magistrate.

When this interview was over, other visitors came,

among whom were a young padre and two students. They came to inquire about the books. The padre seemed disappointed when he found there was none left; but it did not appear whether he wanted one of them for his own use, or whether he wished to discover its heretical tendency, as had been stated by the Cure.

After their departure, Don Manuel came. "Now," thought Gardiner, "does he want me to take back these proscribed books?" The bookseller, drawing his chair close to that of his auditor, and assuming a most portentous seriousness, related the substance of the Curé's sermon; but explained, *that an officer of police had looked at the books, and having pronounced them tò be quite fit for circulation, had declared that the police would not oppose the sale.* Therefore, certain of there being a demand for them, he would take them himself.

Thus a new impetus was given to the circulation of the books. Gardiner judging that, although the Church was very suspicious of Bibles, the State was not so, and that the balance of power lay with the State.

In the evening, to the amazement of Gardiner, the Curé himself entered, accompanied by two other ecclesiastics. He spoke in a most friendly manner, thanked Captain Gardiner for the present he made, said that he should value the books, and concluded by wishing him a happy journey. In a conversation held with his landlady after their departure, it appeared that it was not the Curé, but the Guardian of San Francisco, who had preached in the morning, and had warned the ignorant not to read the books. So this was the meaning of the police officer's argument, that though the people of Buenos Ayres might be intelligent enough to receive the books, the people of Tucuman were too ignorant.

On Monday, a woman called to return a Testament, because the padres had said that, being without notes, it was unfit to read. Don Manuel, however, seemed to have no fear that the sale of Bibles would be impeded, for if some of the poorer classes might return their Testaments, others, especially those in higher stations, would purchase them.

Having succeeded beyond his hopes, Gardiner now commenced his return journey, but on reaching Santiago, was informed by his friend, Don Angelo Carranza, that the sale of Bibles had been impeded by the priests, which account was confirmed by Don José Maria Lopez. The padres had really "prohibited the Bible to the ignorant." Don Angelo went to the Governor to obtain a decisive judgment on the question, whether the Bible was *prohibited to any one or not.* The Governor replied, "It is not prohibited at all." Don Angelo, on hearing this, purchased all the Bibles and Testaments that remained unsold, and immediately, in Gardiner's presence, sold a copy.

It was now clear that there was an opening for the admission of Bibles and religious books among the Spanish-American population of the interior. He had proved that no real power remained to the priests. They might hinder the free circulation of the word of God to some extent, but they could not stop it entirely. They might seize the books of "the ignorant," but could not touch those of "the intelligent." Having ascertained this, and sold his books, Gardiner, much encouraged, travelled homewards.

On his way he heard of the arrest of the post-master at Carnero, who for a long time had been carrying on, unsuspected, a system of robbery. So great was the confidence placed in this Castillanos, that a friend of Gardiner's recommended him to stop at Carnero for the night, on his way to Santiago. A (providential) detention at Cordova, however, had induced him to speed rapidly by the point of danger, and befere his return, Castillanos, with eighty-seven others, was arrested and confined in the jail at Cordova.

While in this wild district, one of the post-masters followed Captain Gardiner, complaining loudly of his presumption in passing *his* house without stopping, and insisted on his turning back, or paying him for his loss. When this produced no effect, the post-master continued his persecuting attendance, and at last threatened to ride with him all the way to Cordova and make a formal complaint to the Governor.

Gardiner thought it not improbable that, being

now in the cut-throat district, an attack might be made upon him, loaded his pistols, and refused to exchange any more words with the persevering post-master. He reached the post-house at Carnero in safety. The new occupant showed great civility, and gave him fresh intelligence of Castillanos, who was still in jail.

A more pleasant scene took place at another post-house, where he stopped to buy bread. The children, to whom on his former journey he had given tracts, now came about the wagon, asking for "libritos, libritos."

On the 30th of December, our traveller reached Cordova, where he was laid up with severe sore-throat and fever. His toilsome journey through the hot, sandy plains, had irritated his complaint, for he would never pause that proper remedies might be applied.

He struggled against the feverish attack which was prostrating him, but was obliged to defer his journey to Buenos Ayres for a fortnight. In vain his friends endeavoured to induce him to give it up altogether, for the present, on account of the disturbed state of the country, where gauchos and Indians were formed into regular pillaging parties. Gardiner's only remark to all this was, "When the time comes for me to proceed, I doubt not that the God of my mercies, who has hitherto so graciously protected me, will prepare the way for me."

As soon as he felt well enough, he determined to

proceed, but he found many hindrances attending his first setting out, and the journey more dangerous than he anticipated. As he advanced, he heard rumours of an attack which had been made, a fortnight before, on La Cruz, by "fifty Christianos," with two hundred Indians. Several were killed on each side. Such is the result of civil war. When the guardians of peace quarrel among themselves, the enemies enter unopposed.

Having arrived safely at Buenos Ayres, Captain Gardiner disposed of his wagon, and without loss of time, embarked for Monte Video, which he also reached in safety, although the passage thither was one of extreme peril. Here he found friends to whom he imparted his plans for introducing Christianity to the heathen, as well as a knowledge of the Bible to those who only knew its truths through the dark lantern of Popery. He was assured that if a Protestant mission were established in Patagonia, he might safely depend on their raising £100 a year from the Protestant congregations at Monte Video, Buenos Ayres, Rio Janeiro, and Valparaiso.

A letter was accordingly written to the Rev. W. Armstrong at Valparaiso, requesting his co-operation, and Captain Gardiner himself returned to England, where he arrived exactly seven months from the time of quitting it.

CHAPTER X.

AN UNSUCCESSFUL ATTEMPT.

"Shouldst not thou also have had compassion on thy fellow-servant, even as I had pity on thee? Matt. xviii. 33.

CAPTAIN GARDINER was not disappointed in his hope of being able to form a society, whose sole object should be the evangelization of those countries he had visited in the interior of South America, beginning at Patagonia. At the end of a few months, a society was formed with an income of £500, and Captain Gardiner embarked with Mr. Robert Hunt, as the Society's first missionary to Patagonia. This gentleman gave up the mastership of an endowed school, when he offered his services to the Society. They very much wished to send out a clergyman, but four years had passed since Captain Gardiner's interview with Wissale, and his promise to return with a missionary; and now fears were entertained that a Chilian settlement, just formed at Port Famine, might exert a fatal influence over Wissale and his people, if further time were lost. Mr. Hunt, therefore, was to remain with Captain Gardiner till he was joined by a clergyman.

The appeal to Valparaiso had been warmly responded to. The Rev. Mr. Armstrong had remitted £200 towards the first year's expenses, one-sixth of which he guaranteed as an annual subscription; and which, no doubt, would have been regularly kept up, but for the untoward events which so soon followed.

Attended by the prayers of the Society and friends of missions, the two Christian adventurers embarked on board the *Rosalie*, which safely traversed the Atlantic, and landed at Oazy Harbour in the Strait of Magellan. They had three small huts, (one for stores, one for cooking, and the other for sleeping,) and every necessary provision for their support for some months. The wandering tribe they came to benefit, were far inland at the time of their arrival, and the *Rosalie*, pursuing her voyage to the Pacific, left them alone. This was in Feb. 1845.

They found the hut of a Fuegian, who with his family seemed inoffensive, and readily showed them where water was to be procured. Two days after landing, Mariano, a deserter from the Chilian fort, arrived. He detailed many adventures and mishaps which he had met with on the way, and declared that he had fallen in with a party of "Bravios Indios," who had robbed and threatened him.

On the same evening, the Fuegian returned with

two companions, and they were at once accused by Mariano as the "Bravios Indios," who had robbed him. To the surprise of Captain Gardiner and Mr. Hunt, the Fuegians, after some demur, admitted the theft, and returned the articles which they had taken.

Mariano also informed them, that Wissale was no longer the wealthy and important chief that he had been; he had lost much of his power and influence, and was wandering about in disgust with a comparatively small number of followers. San Leon (to whom Gardiner had given charge of his tent) was in league with the Chilians of Port Famine; and declared also, that a certain Padre Domingo had begun to teach the Patagonians to become "Catolicos."

This information was by no means agreeable, and our friends, in order to find out the true state of things, locked up two of the huts, leaving the third open, as a shelter to Mariano, and set off in search of the Patagonians. Laden with a gun, some ammunition, and a supply of biscuit, they toiled along the sandy shore, in the direction pointed out by Mariano, and after a time, turning their steps inland, they found traces of the band they sought. After an unsuccessful wandering for four days, Mr. Hunt's strength failed altogether, and Gardiner was obliged to leave him lying on the ground, while he went in search of water. But in this lonely spot, so wild and desolate, while unseen dangers were lurking around, and unexpected difficulties sprang up in their path, it was inspiriting to gaze on the midnight sky, and mark the bold tracing of the glorious Southern Cross.

They had by this time lost all traces of the Patagonians, and therefore retraced their path to the station, which they reached on Saturday, March 8th. Most welcome was the sight of the tent-shaped huts, where they could find shelter at night, and repose on the Sabbath, which was doubly refreshing after their late toil.

In a few days the Patagonians arrived. Wissale came forward in a friendly way, but the first glance at the number of his party confirmed the truth of Mariano's statement. There was the same stalwart chief, armed with the same handsome hunting equipments; but instead of one hundred and twenty horses, he had only ten or twelve, and his followers were but seventy in number. He had grown poor by his intercourse with the Chilians, and San Leon had supplanted him in his own tribe.

As, however, at present, Wissale seemed quiet and peaceable, our friends hoped for the best. He and his family were hungry, but they were now fed to the full.

Mariano had informed Gardiner that when he deserted from the Chilian fort he had a companion named Cruz; that on the way they had quarrelled, and Cruz, joining a party of Patagonians, had remained with them. Gardiner, therefore, wondered where the deserter might be. But like that of many a vicious and reckless being, his presence was felt before he himself was seen. Cruz was in the tent and under the protection of Wissale.

On the next day the chief came, but altogether changed in tone, and seemed determined to pick a quarrel. He satisfied his appetite thoroughly at breakfast, and then requested some biscuits for his children. These were given, by his direction, to a man who stood ready at the door, but no sooner had he disappeared than Wissale repeated the request, on the plea that the man would eat the biscuits just given. As Captain Gardiner declined being trifled with, Wissale made the refusal an excuse for being angry, and wrapping his cloak around him, was in the sulks the whole day.

The man was changed indeed. Some hostile influence was at work. It was easily traced to Cruz. Determined to bring matters to a crisis, Captain Gardiner spoke to the chief in a most conciliating way; and reminding him of his former visit, and the invitation then given him to return with a teacher, stated boldly that he had now come an invited guest, and had brought the teacher. Did Wissale wish them to go or stay? Wissale, not having Cruz at his elbow, said he wished them to stay.

The captain of a merchant ship from Valparaiso for England, coming on shore, was made acquainted with the state of affairs. He spoke to Wissale, and gave him his choice, either to retain and protect Captain Gardiner and Mr. Hunt as friends, or to refuse, and he would take them away in the *Commodore*, which was then at anchor in the bay. Wissale now seemed quite friendly, and desired the Captain to tell the people of England, "that his heart was towards his brother, Captain Gardiner." Had it been possible to have procured a passage to Rio Janeiro in the ship for Mariano and Cruz, all might yet have been well; but on the very day of the *Commodore's* sailing, Wissale returned to his sullen attitude, reserving all his friendship for Cruz. His appetite and demands were alike insatiable. He asked for spirits, tobacco, and food. Once he threatened to use his dirk, and his whole bearing was so hostile that the lives of our friends seemed to hang by a very slender thread. His gusts of ill-temper were sudden and violent, and on one occasion, bringing from his tent some articles which had been given him, threw them disdainfully on the ground, saying that he would not receive anything from either of them.

The *Commodore* was soon followed by the *Ancud* schooner from Port Famine, having on board the Padre Domingo, of whom Mariano had spoken, as being so zealous to win over the Patagonians to the Romish faith. The friar was a South American Indian, trained up on the principle of the Propaganda, as a teacher among the Indian population. He was civil, and so was the captain, offering the

Englishmen a passage to Port Famine, if they wished to go. This, however, was declined, but the growing influence of the Chilian government, and the increasing hostility of Wissale, was so apparent, that Gardiner was convinced that his position was untenable, and our two friends came to the conclusion that it was necessary to abandon Patagonia for the present. On this trying occasion Gardiner writes: "When God hedges up our path, his hand is as conspicuous, and his power and wisdom are to be acknowledged as much, as when he opens to us the widest door of usefulness. 'Shall not the Judge of all the earth do right?' Is it enough for us to know that it is the Lord, and that he never cuts short any work which he has commanded us to undertake, but for some gracious and wise end. What we know not now, we shall know hereafter. We never can do wrong in casting the gospel net on any side, or in any place. During many a dark and wearisome night we may appear to have toiled in vain, but it will not always be so; if we will but wait the appointed time, the promise, though long delayed, will assuredly come to pass. We can know no more than Peter did, at what time, or on what side of the vessel we are most likely to meet with success; but this one word I will add: Having cast the net on one side, let us not slothfully and unbelievingly relinquish the work, but committing ourselves and the heathen, whose souls we seek, afresh to the direction and tender mercy of our covenant God, let us now cast it in humble confidence on the other side; and who can tell but the same gracious Saviour who commanded success to the disciples on the sea of Tiberias, will vouchsafe to ordain strength out of our weakness, so that we shall have cause to admire the riches of his grace, and to exclaim, 'What hath God wrought!'"

Before the schooner left Gregory Bay, the *Ganges* arrived, and being bound for England, our missionary pioneers took their passage home.

How little can we judge of the future from the present! The Chilian settlement has long since been withdrawn from the Strait of Magellan, and with it the active Padre Domingo.

CHAPTER XI.

BOLIVIA.

> "But on he went;
> Mountains and rivers never checked his course,
> Nothing could daunt him."

NOTWITHSTANDING the unsuccessful issue of the attempt to plant a mission in Patagonia, and the great disappointment felt by the supporters of the cause, Gardiner's views of duty did not alter, and he determined again to search for openings among the natives of the interior.

The society had hoped for at least a glimpse of success. They had looked on the offer of Wissale as a real opening, and, unprepared for such a change as had taken place in the character of the chief and position of his tribe, they felt that any further attempt would be a doubtful experiment, upon which they could not expend public money.

Gardiner, however, once more came forward, and with unshaken resolution declared, "the heathen had a right to be instructed in the gospel of Christ." And declaring his intention of going to Terra del

Fuego, he begged the Society to fund the money, and wait to see what would be the result.

This suggestion was adopted, and Captain Gardiner, finding that Mr. Gonzales, a young Spanish Protestant, had been engaged by the committee to go to Patagonia, offered, now that this arrangement was given up, to pay his expenses if he would accompany him. The committee, hearing this, presented him with fifty pounds.

On reaching Monte Video, he found his friends, Dr. Gordon and the Rev. Mr. Armstrong. On inquiring of Dr. Gordon after the fate of the Bibles and Testaments which had been circulated at Cordova, he replied, that the priests had collected together as many as they could, and having been piled in a heap, were burned in presence of all the clergy of the place.

Finding the country about Santa Fé in an unsettled state, Gardiner and Mr. Gonzales went to Valparaiso, from whence they sailed for the port of Cobija, in Bolivia; and Gardiner, having had some French Bibles given him, was able to supply the sailors, most of whom were French, with copies of God's word in their own language.

Having arrived at Cobija, the only port in Bolivia, the two friends prepared for a journey into the interior. Setting forth on a road at first winding, and afterwards broken, which gradually opened out upon a scene of wild Arabian dreariness, they approached Calama, where, having a letter of introduction to Don Ramon Elizalde, they met with much hospitality. Mr. Gonzales being ill from fatigue, it was thought better for him to remain under the kind care of his countryman, for a time, whilst the indefatigable Gardiner proceeded, attended only by a guide. The way to Atacama led through a desert; sometimes, however, the barren waste was enlivened by rose-coloured everlasting flowers, occasional tufts of an aromatic herb, and dark-coloured prickly plants, like the balsam plant of the Falklands. At Atacama, Gardiner was informed that the Indian territory was close to Tarija, that the natives were on good terms with their Spanish-speaking neighbours, and that no missionary had yet visited them. This was confirmed by a traveller who had just returned from that district. Having made preparations for proceeding with as little loss of time as possible, Captain Gardiner was joined by Mr. Gonzales. The journey proved a very troublesome one. The books were warped and injured during the passage through the desert; the bread dried into rusk. The same climate which scorches books, produced venomous beetles called binchucas. But within two days' journey from the desert are forests which abound with the little chinchilla, whose fur is so much admired in England.

Their road lay over a tedious plain of loose stones varied with a few tufts of wiry grass. Sometimes it was so steep and rugged with fragments of rock, that the mules could hardly move forward. The nights were frosty, nevertheless they always slept in the open air, wrapt in blankets, with only one exception, when they took refuge in some low, sepulchral-looking hovels, which were built by the chinchilla hunters.

After six days' toil, they reached Rinconada, in the neighbourhood of which were some gold mines, which had been worked for some distance, but were now abandoned.

The travellers found little rest at Rinconada, where they spent the Sabbath. The Carnival was going on day and night. The whole place was one continued scene of intoxication, dancing, and buffoonery, and the friends were exceedingly annoyed by the piping, drumming, and singing of half-tipsy Indians, until far in the night.

As it was impossible to obtain guides during the Carnival, they were obliged to wait five days. One at last offered, but as it proved that he knew nothing of his business, everything went wrong on the journey to Tarija, which they reached in one month after leaving Cobija.

Here they met with some friends, who gave favourable accounts of the Indians, and told them "they had come to the right place." They likewise informed Gardiner that although a college of the Jesuits was once in the neighbourhood, which had no less than twenty-two missions on the borders of the Chaco, all were now suppressed, not one remained. So the whole country was open to our pioneers.

To follow our travellers very closely in this journey, in which they met with many adventures, might prove fatiguing to our readers, we will therefore refer them to Gardiner's letters, pp. 292—317.

Perhaps in the whole of Gardiner's wanderings he had not encountered such suffering as he experienced in this. Mr. Gonzales became ill; his friend therefore, wishing to visit some Indian villages on the opposite side of the Pilcomayo, the current of which is extremely rapid, was obliged to swim over. But after all his trouble and danger, although kindly received by the natives, the chiefs refused a closer intercourse. Tortured by hosts of flies, wasps, and mosquitoes, with swelled limbs and face, the travellers were obliged to fly before them. On reaching Carapari, Mr. Gonzales was too ill to proceed, and Gardiner, hiring a servant to attend upon him, set off alone to make a visit of inspection into the Indian territory.

Eleven villages were visited, and everywhere a kind reception was given to Captain Gardiner, and a supply of provisions. To every chief he made the same request, that he might be allowed to build a house, dwell among them, and learn their language. He told them he was no Spaniard, but belonged to another nation far away, who had never been at war with them; that he did not wish to deprive them of any of their land; that whatever provisions were supplied to himself and friends should be paid for; and that he would bring some presents for the chiefs. Hitherto the opposition to the residence of a foreigner among them had proved insurmountable. Various were the excuses: one chief had only food enough for himself and family, a second chief referred him to a third, the third recommended him to apply to a fourth, but the refusal had been unanimous. The last attempt in this district was now to be made.

It was Sunday; and under the broad shade of a forest tree, Captain Gardiner knelt apart from the Indian villagers, and poured out his heart to God, and told all his difficulties.

With much patience Captain Gardiner continued his researches, but "the neighbouring chiefs did not wish any *Christian* to reside within their district." He returned, therefore, to Carapari, and attended upon his sick friend; but a fever prevailing there, he became ill himself, and decided on leaving that place, hoping to reach San Luis in the intervals of the attack, the fever being of an intermittent character.

After a painful journey, in which more than once, being perfectly helpless, he was obliged to lie down under a tree; and suffering the most intense torment of thirst, without having water to assuage it, they reached San Luis, where Captain Gardiner was attacked with dysentery, which brought him almost to the borders of the grave. But as he says himself, "Never was that gracious promise more fully verified, 'As thy day is, so shall thy strength be,' than in this journey." Removed into the purer air of San Luis, the friends recovered.

Gardiner had a most satisfactory interview with the Governor of Bolivia, in which the latter, after hearing the object and plans of our missionary pioneers, not only approved, but promised to lend his influence in the Congress in their behalf.

Meeting with further approval at Tarija, Gardiner recovered his usual high spirits, but this happy state was not long to continue. In the month of August, letters were received from the British Consul at Chuquisaca, which assured him, "that the Romish clergy were all up in arms at the attempt of a heretic to convert the Indians of the Tarija frontier to the heterodox doctrines of Protestantism," and advised him to give up the attempt as impracticable. "All labour," said he, "in the Lord's vineyard, in this country, must be done with Roman Catholic tools, as in this republic (Bolivia) *Romanism* alone will be permitted." Nevertheless, he determined to go to Chuquisaca and have an interview with the president, who, probably, did not fully understand his plans. On the way he met the propio from Chuquisaca with their letters.

Their petition had been referred to Congress, but was now returned with a negative affixed to it. By the same letter, he heard of the sudden death of Mr. Masterton, the British Consul.

Gardiner, having advised with his San Luis friends on the propriety of submitting a modified petition to the Minister of the Interior, was, by them, introduced to that officer, who, after reading it, seemed to think there could be no objection to its contents. From thence they went to the president's, who declared he would not oppose the petition, as he would have acceded to the former one but for the existing laws.

Setting apart a day (Oct. 3d) for fasting and prayer, this devoted servant of the cross prepared himself to meet the issue with calmness, let it be what it might. On October 7th, while on his way to the minister's office, he met his friend, Don Sebastian, who had kindly come to inform him, that the president had notified to him, while in Congress, that the petition respecting the Indians had received his sanction.

Joy now once more sprung up in the heart of Captain Gardiner. He thought the way was at last opened for missionary work among the Indians, and concluded it would be best for Mr. Gonzales to remain in South America and secure the important steps just gained, while he returned to England in order to report progress, and send out a missionary to join his friend, who proposed to continue, in the mean time, at Potosi, and acquire the Quichua language. He arrived in England, after an absence of sixteen months, and the Society, encouraged by the cheering prospect, sent out Mr. Robles, another Spanish Protestant, to aid in the preliminary work of the mission.

But whilst he was on his way, another revolutionary movement took place in Bolivia, which ended in the deposition of the friendly president. Thus the difficulties were renewed, for, when the governing power was withdrawn, the influence of the priests was in the ascendant. And the Society at home, not feeling able to maintain an infant mission in the midst of the confusion which attends on civil troubles, reluctantly gave the order to the two agents to withdraw from the station at present.

CHAPTER XII.

THE RECONNOITRING PARTY.

"To hallowed duty,
Here with a loyal and heroic heart,
Bind we our lives."

FROM the time of Captain Gardiner's first and unsuccessful attempt to form a mission station at Gregory Bay, he entertained the idea of going to Terra del Fuego. Having succeeded beyond his expectation in making an opening for usefulness in Bolivia, he now pressed upon the committee of the Society of Missions to Patagonia and South America the practicability of commencing a mission to Terra del Fuego. His appeal, however, was coldly received; there was little attraction in the barren island of Fuegia, with its few hungry barbarians, to interest those whose sympathies can only lay hold of magnificent projects. But the subject had taken such a firm hold of his heart and imagination, that he was not to be baffled. His zeal in the cause, his untiring efforts to raise the necessary funds by his own efforts, after many cold looks and chilling receptions, at length awakened some sympathy, and when he proposed that an attempt should be made on a small scale, which, whether successful or not, would, at least, be a step in the right direction and result in improved information, they consented. He proposed to take four sailors and one ship-carpenter, with one decked boat, a dingey, a whale boat, and two wigwam huts, with supplies for six months, and establish a station. Staten Island, which lies east of the most easterly point of Fuegia, was the place selected as the scene of this experiment. The Committee consented, the preparations were made, the men engaged, among whom was Joseph Erwin, a ship-carpenter; and when the *Clymene* barque sailed for Peru, she bore the reconnoitring party on their arduous service. They sighted Staten Island at the close of the ninth week, but the weather was so tempestuous, that no landing could be effected, until the ship anchored at Lennox Harbour. Our reconnoitring party now determined to try their boat, and landed on Picton Island, where they remained all night. In the morning Gardiner read the thirty-fifth chapter of Isaiah aloud; all knelt down for family prayer, and then, proceeding with their observation of the island, selected a spot for a station. The harbour was named Banner Cove.

The return trip to the *Clymene* was both difficult and dangerous. The weather was squally, with sleet and hail; the boat leaked and required frequent baling out. Wet, weary, and in danger, the fearless little band beat about for fifteen hours, at the end of which time, they ran for Lennox Island, where they landed on a sandy beach, tolerably well sheltered. After a great deal of trouble, they kindled a fire, but did not erect the tent, sleeping between the folds of a tarpaulin on the beach.

For breakfast they ate their last biscuit; and as the weather was too tempestuous to permit them going by sea, they stowed away the furniture of their boat, and after reading the twenty-first Psalm, united in prayer and set off on a difficult journey overland.

The way led through bog and forest, now traversing hill and dale; here assisted by an Indian-path, then forcing a way through tangled trees and brushwood. At length the cheering "Sail, ho!" was joyfully cried out by one of the party, and there, indeed, was the old *Clymene* quietly lying at anchor.

They kindled a fire, but it was long before any notice was taken of it. When it was seen, the captain, who had been looking for his late passengers by sea and not by land, sent off a boat to ascertain whether it was kindled by Fuegians or not. As the boat approached the shore, the rowers gave a loud shout and fired a gun, which salute was joyfully returned by our friends.

In the morning, some Fuegians visited the ship, and afterwards, while Gardiner and his men were erecting their store-house, another party arrived.

They did not seem decidedly hostile, but were so mischievous and thievish that it was necessary to be continually on the watch, in order to preserve the store-house. It was impossible to keep the natives out of the dwelling-house. They made signs for their hosts to lie down and go to sleep, evidently wishing to carry off the property, while the owners were off their guard. While Gardiner was writing some memoranda, a Fuegian entered, and taking up the inkstand, poured the whole contents on the unfinished page. They were, therefore, obliged to keep on their guard, not daring to separate even for shooting or fishing; besides, dreading that if the number of Fuegians should be reinforced, they should be plundered of all their provisions. It, therefore, became a very serious question whether it would be possible to form a mission station on shore; and Gardiner, with a heavy heart, decided on abandoning the spot for the present. Before re-embarking with their tent, house, and boats, they landed a couple of goats, planted some garden-seeds, and took their leave of the place, hoping, under more favourable auspices, to visit it again.

Keenly disappointed, Captain Gardiner retired to his cabin in the *Clymene*, and thought over many plans; the only one which promised likely to prove successful, was the following. He writes: "There is but one sure and successful method of combating the grievous difficulty, which alone obstructs a free and profitable intercourse with these barbarous people. . . . A Fuegian mission must of necessity be afloat, or, in other words, a mission vessel moored in the stream, must be substituted for a mission-house erected on the shore. A large vessel would not be required. I should recommend a ketch or brigantine, of one hundred and twenty tons with a master and ten hands, with provisions for twelve months; three-fourths of which should be deposited at the Falklands. Further supplies should be forwarded there from England and placed in charge of an agent appointed for the purpose. It would be advisable that the mission vessel should call every three months at the Falklands, in order to forward and receive letters, etc., to and from England. . . . The expenses incurred, during the stay of the vessel in that colony, in providing the crew with beef and vegetables, might be covered by disposing of timber brought from Picton Island, and which might be kept felled in readiness to be shipped." In conclusion he asks, "Can we, with any consistency as Christians, having, as it were, lifted the latch and crossed the threshold, turn back at the very point when we should advance, dismayed at the cost it would entail, and the sacrifices that must be made, although the everlasting condition of immortal souls is involved in the question. Let us not be weary in well doing, for in due time we shall reap if we faint not."

On reaching Payta, the mission property was sold, and arrangements made for the seamen to proceed to England. Gardiner, however, remained behind for a month, in order to make another journey of inquiry as to the facilities for introducing Bibles and tracts into the country. He learned that two missions were in operation among the independent Indians, under the direction of the Ecuador government, but also found that the state of education was at a very low ebb among the Spanish population. A lady inquired of him, whether Europe was not a little on this side of Spain. A curé asked him if London was not a part of France; and much surprised to hear that Britain was an island, inquired whether it was an island in the sea. Another person of good station inquired about Jerusalem, and supposed the chief part of English trade was with Jerusalem; and asked if Constantinople were still in existence. He had, however, some interesting conversations on the subject which lay nearest his heart. His host at Palo Blanco was an old man, and at the time of Gardiner's arrival, was reading a summary of Scripture history. A conversation commenced, in which the old man said he had a New Testament which was printed at Paris, and when his guest spoke of those published in England, he observed that they were prohibited, as many of the words were altered. Gardiner explained the difference to his satisfaction. He thought, with respect to the adoration of the Virgin Mary, that it was well she should plead with her son, but when the doctrine of the Bible was stated, he said,

"If this be so, our petitions should be made directly to the Saviour."

Determined to leave nothing undone, Captain Gardiner called at the house of both the curés. Finding the youngest abroad, he made known his errand to some persons in the house, and left an "Auxillo" (a tract compiled of texts of Scripture). The other padre was at home, and appeared much gratified at the present of a tract, and on our pioneer's referring to the Bible from which the several texts contained in it were taken, he stated (as the landlord had previously done), that there was not one in the place. Never supposing that in this confession he included himself, Captain Gardiner asked whether he had a Bible in Spanish; when, to the surprise of his questioner, he acknowledged, that neither he nor his coadjutor had a copy either in Spanish or Latin. "Were Bibles prohibited?" he asked. "No," was the reply, "there was no obstacle of that kind, but they were very scarce." He seemed to feel that it was a great pity there was such a dearth of the word of God.

Gardiner had an earnest conversation with the sub-curé, who paid him a visit. He confessed that he had never seen a Bible, but only some extracts from it, as used in their services. He asked whether the Protestants had the rite of baptism among them; whether they had bishops, and whether they were consecrated by the Pope. He was answered, that the rite of baptism was used as commanded in the Bible; that the bishops consecrated each other, that there was nothing about the Pope in the Bible, that Jesus Christ alone was Head of the Church. He then inquired, "Who has the keys?" Gardiner answered, "No man. The word of God alone opens and shuts; and whatever is not in conformity with God's word will not stand; the Pope cannot change the words of the Bible." The curé took these remarks very good humouredly, and told our friend he "ought to come and live there." Gardiner promised to send him a Bible, by the study of which he would know whether all he had said was true or not. Soon after this, Captain Gardiner proceeded to England, and took an early opportunity of sending the Bibles he had promised to Peru, and their arrival was acknowledged with thanks.

CHAPTER XIII.

SURGEON WILLIAMS.

"Oh speed on the morn,—Lord, thy promise fulfil,
Pierce the gloom with thy brightness,—thy Spirit instil.
E'en now cause some beams of the forthcoming day
On Andes' cold turrets to flicker and play,
Till the sun in his strength bid the shadows decay."

WHILST Gardiner was prosecuting his labours among the independent Indians of South America, another mind was maturing in England, which at its full development would fit its possessor for the task of a pioneer missionary. Richard Williams was the second son of Mr. Rice Williams, of Dursley, Gloucestershire, and was born there on the 15th of May, 1815.

In his childhood he evinced great tenderness of feeling, but with that ardent and affectionate disposition there were frequent outbreaks of a passionate temper, and his strong determination amounted to obstinacy. He gave no indications of piety, but in the transparency and truthfulness of his character might be perceived the germ of future excellence.

For if little can be hoped from a childhood where deceit is the constitutional sin, it is seldom but the boy attains to something noble, who "cannot tell a lie."

At school, his teacher remarked that there "was something in him which distinguished him from the mass of common boys; there was a character about him even then, which indicated purpose, and good in the future, and abilities which only required to be guided into a proper channel to make him a useful man." His father intended him to be a mechanic, and there were many facilities for his obtaining worldly prosperity. But he did not like the monotonous employment; he would be a doctor, and not a plane-maker. All the money he could procure, and all the hours he could spare, were given to studies bearing on the medical profession. An uncle who had acquired a reputation in making carpenters' planes, bequeathed his thriving business to his nephew, on condition that the profits of the first ten years should be shared with his sisters. It was a kind arrangement, and gave the young man a good opportunity to make his own fortune, and to provide for his father's family. But he had other aspirations. His elder brother was surgeon on board an English vessel, the *Owen Glendower*, and Richard, encouraged by his example, and perhaps haunted by the brilliant precedent of the Hunters, resolved to imitate the young journeyman, who quitted the carpenter's bench to become the prince of anatomists, and the collector of a world-famed museum. But the brothers Williams were not destined to repeat the romance of the Hunters. The elder, a generous and noble-hearted young man, died at Madras; and for Richard, God had provided something better than scientific reputation. Our friend, besides this professional bias, delighted in reading books, and sometimes dreamed of making them. By great exertions he accomplished a medical course, and having studied at University College, and at the London Hospital, as well as having been initiated in the practical details of his profession by a cousin in Oxfordshire, he was able to pass his examination in May, 1841, when twenty-six years of age. For some time he acted as assistant to several medical gentlemen at Norwich and elsewhere, and eventually, his brother-in-law and sister, Mr. and Mrs. Hill, being resident at Burslem, Staffordshire, sent him an invitation to come and settle beside them. That invitation he accepted; and by the success with which his first cases were treated, he soon attracted notice, and became a popular practitioner, and a field of abundant occupation was opening before him. Distinguished as he was by his skill in the noble profession he had chosen, he was even more so by the purity of his character; and was held up by many as a model worthy of imitation. But notwithstanding his moral purity, and gentle and prepossessing manners, he was entirely without religion. Warm-hearted and manly, he was not devout; and amidst all his solicitude for the bodily health of his neighbours, the salvation of their souls or of his own, had never cost him a thought. With an ardent and enthusiastic temperament, he had no love for his heavenly Friend, and no sympathy with that philanthropy which seeks the eternal welfare of its objects.

One Sunday, a friend found him in his office reading a newspaper; and asked him if this was a right employment of the Lord's day. His answer was, "Were my mind, like yours, satisfied that Christianity is true, I would embrace it with all my soul, and I would live accordingly." His visitor felt that he was sincere, and could only regret that, to a nature so energetic, and in many respects so ingenuous, the gospel was nothing more than a cunning fable; and, as he himself declared, the Bible, so far as his perusal of it went, "was a mere lumber book." Believing in God, as a Being infinitely wise and just, and adoring his excellency as revealed in his beautiful and magnificent works, he had until this time no belief in Christianity, but regarded it as an absurdity, and its votaries deluded. He denied the innate corruption of man, and deified human nature as capable of transcendent virtue. He hoped that the soul was immortal, but never felt convinced that it was so; and as to the existence of a devil and everlasting torments, he viewed the doctrine as a defamation of the justice of God, and believed it no more than a bugbear.

This state, however, was not to continue; the same Spirit which enkindled light in the mind of the great Apostle of the Gentiles, revealed to him the darkness in which his soul was enveloped, and his conviction was powerful, and his conversion striking. The Bible, hitherto a sealed book, was now a river of water to his thirsty soul. The bright, revealing light made its truths perfectly clear; he read it as the word of God, and resolved to make it the rule of his life. He speaks of the first period of this change as being a foretaste of heavenly peace. Holiness, with its celestial gilding, seemed to tinge every object which surrounded him. The Saviour was precious to him, and his soul was filled with joy. He wondered at his former darkness, and was amazed that he had never been able to perceive the precious light that had so long been shining in his way. But notwithstanding all this joy, there were times of occasional depression, such as every true Christian has experienced on entering upon the new track, and for which he could not account. He believed that the work of renovation had been so fully completed, that he never could, wilfully, sin against God again. Darkness surrounded him, he felt that sin still palpably abounded in his heart; he saw how great was the inherent corruption and original depravity of the human soul, and great was the bitterness of the moment of this discovery. But he did not relapse into his first cold estate; but remaining prayerful, although sad, he found it was only the first of a series of painful but important lessons, which, (to use his own words,) "convinced me that God had only hitherto instructed me in the first principles, and laid the foundation for my faith; but that the work of grace had to be carried on, and an absolute change of heart effected, by many a severe and fiery ordeal."

At length, however, the warfare came less painful, and the peace promised to the true believer, stole insensibly over his soul. Retiring from the whirl and confusion of business, to the beautiful and quiet scenery of North Wales, whither he had been advised to go on account of his health, his mind, which had been greatly disturbed by a severe nervous disease, recovered its tone, and his body its usual vigour. As he contemplated the glorious works of the great Creator, as revealed in the grandeur of Snowdon, and the charms of Llanberis, he felt that the God of nature and the God of revelation were one, and he began more sensibly to feel the relation wherein we stand to the Great Ruler, by the conjoint link of creation and redemption. He, the creature of his hand, could, through the Redeemer, look up and believe that the Power which guided the planets in their course, would direct him in all his ways, and preserve him with providential care. He now was able to discern how great was the love of God towards the world, in giving his only begotten Son, that whosoever believeth in him should not perish, but have everlasting life. He felt that it is the First and the Last who there expresses his care for the whole family of man, even to the most insignificant individual; and filled with wonder and adoration at that mercy, and love, and grace, humbled himself before Him.

CHAPTER XIV.

CHRISTIAN EXPERIENCE AND USEFULNESS.

"Truth from the earth, like to a flower,
Shall bud and blossom then;
And justice from her heavenly bower,
Look down on mortal men."

"No soul can soar too loftily whose aim
Is God-given truth, and brother love of man."

It has been said that there is a certain temperament, and there are mental tendencies, from which, if a man is not content to remain a Presbyterian in Scotland, or an Episcopalian in England, it may be predicted which other section of the Christian community he will join. The Wesleyan body is the great absorbent of warm hearts and fervent spirits. In the frequency of its devotional meetings, in the frankness and unreserve of its Christian intercourse, in the vigour of its responses and the soaring rapture of its hymns, and in the benevolent vivacity which finds a post and an employment for every member, it meets many cravings of the young and ardent convert. It is not therefore to be wondered at that one of such an impulsive and ardent temperament as Mr. Williams, should, after his conversion, join the Methodist church. For twelve months previous to his great change, although, as we have already stated, very careless on the subject of religion, he had attended divine service at the Wesleyan chapel, owing to the esteem he entertained for the ministers then labouring in the circuit. Nevertheless, as he says himself, "in those days I would have scorned the thought as an insult to my understanding, had it been suggested that I might at some day join the Methodist society. For them, of all sects, I had the greatest distaste, and they were a by-word and a reproach in my mouth." However, when he had opportunities of judging more closely, he arrived at a much more elevated opinion of their Christian integrity and worth than he had formerly entertained. He found their fervent zeal for the cause of God most attractive to his now roused feelings. He desired that every creature should rejoice in the glorious tidings revealed to himself, and could have wished for a trumpet tongue, to echo salvation over the length and breadth of the earth. In this spirit he therefore presented himself at one of the class-meetings, and received a ticket on trial. But all was not yet light within his soul. Most severe were the spiritual conflicts through which he passed; various temptations came in his way; his soul was often filled with darkness deep as midnight; he was often assailed by doubts of the truth, and was frequently on the point of giving up all in despair.

The secret of these distressing feelings was not then known to him. He had hitherto been trusting in his own strength, and had not recollected how, without the aid of God's Holy Spirit, he could not perform one duty aright. There was, however, an inward sincerity of heart in seeking after God, and after a time of sore conflict, in which pride was completely conquered, light was once more poured into his soul. He felt with comfort and delight that the Captain of salvation was with him in the contest; the grace which he coveted was granted, and the career of Mr. Williams was henceforth marked by warm, consistent, and sincere piety. His profession, in which he was exceedingly popular, gave him many opportunities of doing good among the poor; and on such occasions he never failed to urge on their attention the interests of their never-dying souls. Thus, long before he had thoughts of labouring abroad, he had become a medical missionary at home. In the year when Burslem was visited by the cholera, the success of his treatment entailed on him enormous labour: but even amidst all the toil and hurry of that anxious season he found time to pray with the sick, and to point them to the Lamb of God who taketh away the sin of the world. One other field of his usefulness must not be forgotten. He was in the habit of visiting the barracks at Burslem, and distributing tracts to the soldiers. In two instances, at least, he succeeded in awakening religious impressions; and those men still maintain their steadiness. After he left Burslem, Mr. Williams kept up a correspondence with one of them. Thus gradually drawn into the work of a home missionary, Mr. Williams enjoyed it exceedingly. It was an outlet for all the energies of his eager and benevolent nature, and the impression frequently produced, was a delightful recompense, and cheered him to proceed. He began to feel that in such labours he would fain "spend and be spent," and belonging to a community in which evangelistic effort has been an almost invariable result from personal piety, it is not wonderful that his thoughts began to be directed toward the missionary enterprise. Just as his thorough-going enthusiasm at a former period had forced its way from the workshop to the college, so now the same fervour, intensified and consecrated, was urging him out into the field of the world: and, although in a quarter little expected, a door was about to open.

We have already stated how Captain Gardiner had made repeated journeys of exploration at great personal hazard among the South American Indians, in the hope of discovering an opening for the introduction of the gospel, but found them so suspicious of strangers, and on every side so hemmed in by Spanish Popery, that he was convinced that nothing could be effected among them at that time.

One region, however, appeared more promising. There were no Romish priests in Patagonia and scarcely any European settlements, and accordingly, as has already been shown, he there made a trial, but, owing to the slender means at his disposal, had found it impossible to persevere. Undaunted by repeated disappointments, and with his heart full of interest for the South American Indians, Gardiner would allow his friends no rest till they gave him a fair and final opportunity. Far away as Fuegia was, and few as were its hungry barbarians, he unweariedly pleaded their importance. Guiana excepted, of all that mighty continent, no other spot was so accessible to Protestant missions. It was the Gibraltar of the South Pacific, and it was of no small consequence to our mariners to people, with friendly occupants, the Straits of Magellan and the coasts in the rear of Cape Horn. Above all, it was the only avenue attainable to the vast tribes of the interior—the tenants of the Andes, and the fierce nomads of the Pampas. As Popery had closed the main gates against the gospel, it was of paramount urgency to seize and keep open this postern. The representations of this heroic evangelist again produced their impression, and his own self-devotion was more affecting than argument. He put his life into the venture; others gave their money. One lady contributed a thousand pounds; a new committee was constructed, and circulars were issued; still it seemed impossible to raise money for the execution of Gardiner's original scheme, and instead of a brigantine he proposed to take two launches. Two launches were built, the one as a floating mission-house, the other as a store-ship and magazine, with two small boats as tenders. An advertisement was inserted in the religious newspapers inviting catechists to join the expedition, and this meeting the eye of Mr. Williams, he offered his services to Captain Gardiner. This offer was favourably received, the committee were satisfied as to Mr. Williams's personal worth and general qualifications; and, having passed an examination in theology satisfactorily, he was appointed, along with Mr. Maidment, a catechist in the Fuegian Mission. In taking this step, Mr. Williams relinquished a good income, and postponed for a long period some cherished prospects. To one of his tender and affectionate spirit, the trial of parting with so many loved friends and relatives was particularly severe. But he had little time to spare for sorrowful musings, for before he could dispose of his practice, or go to bid farewell to some of his nearest kindred, the time of embarkation arrived, and it required his best speed to reach Liverpool before the sailing of the *Ocean Queen*.

CHAPTER XV.

FUEGIA.

"Self-devoted to the Lord
  Home's sweet comforts they resign;
Trusting in his holy word,
  On his promise they recline,—
Not in vain,—their vessel brings
Bounties from the King of kings."

On Saturday, September 7th, 1850, the *Ocean Queen*, bound for San Francisco, hauled out of the basin and stood out for the wide ocean. Fairly on board, and gazing on the vast expanse before him, how varied were the emotions which filled the heart of Richard Williams! But,—as he tells us in the journal, which he kept not only on the voyage but afterwards at Fuegia, and which, the companion of his wanderings, and confidant of all his musings, has survived many perils, and been sent home to his family,—the one above all others, was a sense of joy at the certainty of now being actually engaged in the great work of making known the Saviour of the world; and that, too, to a poor benighted race of savages. Now, for the first time, he met those who were to be his companions in the work of faith. Besides Captain Gardiner, there was Mr. Maidment the catechist; Joseph Erwin, the faithful ship-carpenter, who had before been to Patagonia with Gardiner; the three boatmen from Cornwall, Pearce, Badcock, and Bryant, who had worked together as fishermen, and lived together as Christians. All were cheerful and happy, although they had parted on that day from all they loved, and the land of their birth. It was not the cheerfulness of resignation, but the cheerfulness of brave men, who have coolly made up their minds to dare anything for Christ's sake.

Everything went on most harmoniously with the little mission party; the voyage, up to the fifth of November, had been a very fair one; they were delayed for a considerable length of time, by variable winds and calms as they approached the Line; but had had no rough weather. Three of their party were taken down with fever, which gave them some ground for anxiety, yet all recovered remarkably. "In their affliction," says Mr. Williams, "the different characters of the three young men were strikingly exhibited, but all gave evidence that they were well fitted for the work they had undertaken."

The vessel was to land the mission party at Picton Island, and now, having become somewhat leaky, it was necessary to overhaul her; therefore Gardiner, who intended to profit by this unavoidable delay, proposed, by the help of the crew, to dig an entrenchment around the site of their future residence, and inside of this to raise up high walls all around. As soon as the *Ocean Queen* left Picton Island, the mission party would sail on a voyage of discovery, going, among other places, to Woollya, a place where Jemmy Button, a Fuegian taken to England by Captain Fitzroy, was left, on his return from England, after a three years' absence. Gardiner hoped to be able to persuade him or some of his relations to locate beside them; but if unsuccessful in the endeavour, they would go still farther to the west, in order to obtain two or three boys from a different tribe, and retain them for the purpose of learning their language. Two months after the departure of the *Ocean Queen* with the brave band of Christian pioneers from England, the Committee having received encouraging letters from the hopeful Gardiner, prepared to send out a second six-months' supply of provisions, and every effort was used to find a vessel to take it. They were, however, unable to accomplish this purpose; no vessel would take the stores there, and therefore, fell back upon the advice which Gardiner had given them before he sailed, to send stores to the Falklands, thence to be forwarded by a vessel, which he had reason to believe was sent monthly by the government for wood to Terra del Fuego. This information was confirmed by what appeared to be authentic sources, and the stores were, therefore, put on board the brig *Pearl*, which was to sail for that colony in April.

On Friday, November 29th, they had a sight of the mountains of Fuegia, but at a great distance. The voyage was now nearing its close, and on the evening of this day, our pioneer's hearts were cheered by a brilliant flood of light from the setting sun, which, as Williams says, "greatly encouraged their hearts," taking it as an earnest that we shall not be altogether wanting in bright days and sunny visitations, and likewise deeming it in our fancies as a welcome paid us by Fuegia's luminary.

At half-past four, Gardiner announced that the land was well in sight. Mr. Williams arose and went on deck. The snow-tipped mountains of Fuegia were looming through the vapours of the morning sky, and the rugged land threw a faint, cold smile upon the shivering party, who now came forward to meet her rough, but they hoped welcome greeting. At eight o'clock they were off the Strait of Le Maire, but the wind being adverse, they could not take advantage of the tide; consequently they had to lie off, and beat between the two coasts of Staten Island and the main land. They had thus abundant opportunity for seeing this remarkable land, and likewise abundant experience of the extreme disagreeableness of the neighbourhood of the Strait of Le Maire. The gale blowing strong from the S. E., the white spray dashing about in the wildest manner, sudden puffs of wind, with ominous gathering of dark clouds, and a chilly aspect of the whole heavens, with sudden gusts of snow, or thin driving sleet, with occasional liftings of the mist, and a few glimmering rays of sunshine burnishing the snowy sides of the mountains, continued throughout the whole day, and gave our pioneers an ample experience of Fuegian weather. It must be confessed that if it was a sample, it was none of the best. In excellent keeping with the rough and wintry climate is the aspect of the land. Words can never do justice to its frowning, wild, and wintry character. Staten Island is unequalled as a place of dreariness and forlorn solitude. Its bare, broken, jagged, turret-like hills, present the idea of an immense fortress, erected by nature herself, and seem to frown back all attempts on the part of man to disturb her. Altogether of volcanic origin, it seems from a distance as though it were clad in some hard and impenetrable covering, and, saving the snows on its ridges and slopes, of one uniform russet-brown colour. It is no wonder that it has never been inhabited. Our devoted little band were however not disturbed by the gloom of these surroundings, for the light of God's countenance poured in upon the soul, reflects its own light, and irradiates all around. Wrapped up in their cloaks, although confined in the cabin, and suffering from the continual rolling and pitching of the ship, they were yet hopeful and cheerful. Mr. Williams says in his journal, "Surely Fuegia is the land of darkness, the country of gloom; a scene of wild desolation, both land and climate agree as to character, the one frowning and desolate, the other black and tempestuous. A few, and only a few, cheering smiles has the sun beamed upon us, and the cold snows upon the rough masses of Staten Island put on an unnatural appearance, and looked more and more pale under the reviving influences of the light. If such the land, and such the climate, we have reason to expect the people will not fall short of congruity with either. Well, how do I bear up under these not very flattering prospects? Have I been taken unawares? No. Have I been disappointed? No. The hour has come; and though I have never painted to my mind all that I should have to encounter, yet I am not any the less unprepared for the trial, because I have not to grapple with it in my own strength, nor to prepare myself for the encounter. I verified this whilst reading the twelfth chapter of Romans. God's Holy Spirit engaged my soul in fervent prayer for grace to help me. I was led to offer up my body as a living sacrifice unto God, and with my whole heart consenting, with my entire will prostrate and subjected to the will of God, that I might prove what is his good, and acceptable, and perfect will. I surrendered myself into the hand of Jesus, with so complete a trust in him and love to him, as it was delightful to feel; and experienced a sensible manifestation of God to my soul, accepting my offer."

After beating about from the 29th of November to the 5th of December, exposed to danger, and the men harassed at their duties from drifting snow-squalls and huge seas like cascades pouring their volumes of water upon them, they at last arrived at their destination, and cast anchor in Banner Roads. The night had been very foggy, with a heavy drizzling rain; but clearing up before they anchored, which was at nine in the morning. While drifting off Picton Island, they saw three canoes, which presently put off for the ship, each one containing a Fuegian and his family. Though scarcely discernible with the naked eye, they vociferated, "Yammer schooner," (Give me,) which is their invariable answer to all questions. They also saw five goats perched among the rocks, two of which, the crew, on going ashore, caught; one of them proving to be the original Nanny, brought from England by Captain Gardiner on a former voyage. He presented her to the Captain of the *Ocean Queen*. The appearance of the people as the boats hove near, made an indelible impression on all of the ship's company. It seemed incredible they could be human beings. They observed a lapsided thing on the water, not to be called a boat, or realizing their ideas of a canoe, but so deep that the heads only of the Fuegians could be seen in it. As these dark masses of hair, like so many mops, drew nearer, and the features were discernible, the expression seemed to create general surprise. "In many of them," says Mr. Williams, "on a nearer inspection, indeed I may say in all, the lineaments of the noblest humanity, and features expressive of benevolence and generosity were present, though as it were, buried deep in deplorable ignorance and abject want. One woman had a remarkably prepossessing countenance, very open and cheerful; so had one of the men, and we were encouraged accordingly. I had taken some comfort to my mind from the favourable aspect which the surrounding islands presented; but now my heart swelled with emotion, full of pleasure and satisfaction that our errand was for the purpose of imparting benefits so great and so much needed to these poor creatures. I hailed the prospect with a degree of rapture." Such was the cheerful spirit with which our pioneers surveyed the field of their destined labours. But we are forced to remark, they made its acquaintance under very great advantages. Being December, it was the antarctic midsummer; and like the climate, the natives wore their best faces. They wanted food and trinkets from the strangers; and as long as their visitors remained on ship-board they were safe from tricks and violence. But before proceeding with the narrative, it may be well to introduce the reader to the place and people. We shall thus better understand how arduous was the task which these pious pilgrims had undertaken, and shall be able to sympathize more fully in the great fight of afflictions which they were soon to pass through.

CHAPTER XVI.

THE LAND OF DARKNESS.

"O'er the gloomy hills of darkness,
Cheered by no celestial ray,
Sun of righteousness! arising,
Bring the bright, the glorious day.
Send the gospel
To the earth's remotest bound."

THE outline of South America may be compared to a paper kite; and, like a kite, there is attached to its apex a jointed tail, of which Fuegia and the South Shetlands are the only fragments seen above water. As seen on a school-room map, Terra del Fuego is a dim islet, deriving its chief importance from its famous headland, Cape Horn. On a nearer inspection, however, this nebulous patch resolves itself into a cluster of islands; one very large, surrounded with a crowd of smaller attendants; and far from the main land stands the kerbstone of the New World—Cape Horn, with his surf-beaten pyramid. Although heretofore considered as only the fag-end of America, and in that vast continent regarded but as the last of the caudal vertebræ of the Alps, if found in Europe, Terra del Fuego would be a country of some consideration. Its second-rate islands are larger than the Isle of Wight or the Isle of Man, and the surface of its mainland is equal to the lowlands of Scotland. It has received its name of Fuego, or the land of fire, from its volcanic origin, so plainly developed in the whole rugged outline. Steep and craggy rocks thrown everywhere in wild irregularity; mountains rising to a height of six or seven thousand feet, with glaciers coming down to the sea, and its frowning skies, render it one of the most dreary and inhospitable regions of the globe. In a latitude corresponding to Edinburgh, the sky seldom clears, and the rainy squalls of summer are the only relief from the sleet and snow of winter. Nothing, however, in the Northern Hemisphere, could give a fac-simile of a Fuegian *williwaw*. This ferocious wind is capable of overturning almost every obstacle; and, like grass in a swathe, not only branches but whole trees will sometimes be found piled up at the mouth of a gully, where its rough sickle had passed. Notwithstanding its boisterous summers and its perpetual storms, the average temperature of Fuegia is about the same as Quebec or Montreal; and it is said that the people of London have days as cold as any which occur in Hoste or the Navaien Islands. The range between the extremes of heat and cold is small, and this comparative equality, along with the abundant moisture, is favourable to certain varieties of vegetation; for instance, the fuchsia, which is almost everywhere a conservatory plant, grows wild in Fuegia, and with another plant, in Europe equally delicate, *Veronica decussata*, becomes a tree with a trunk half a foot in diameter. The potato, although indigenous to the adjacent mainland, has not been found in these islands; celery, a species of currant, the berry of an arbutus, and one kind of mushroom, are the only esculents. The characteristic vegetation is two sorts of beech-tree; one (*Fagus betuloides*) is an evergreen; the other (*Fagus Antarctica*) is deciduous. Unless discouraged by the thinness of soil spread over the granitic rocks, these trees occur everywhere, and if not stunted by the winds, attain a goodly size. No one can imagine how little charm is to be found in the scenery of Fuegia, except those who have spent weeks among the pines of the Black Forest, or the arbor vitæ swamps of the Mississippi, and understand what an incubus on the spirit a monotonous vegetation becomes. Land animals are few, even insects are rare, and there are but few flies and beetles; like Ireland, Fuegia is exempt from serpents and even frogs. The most important quadruped is the guanaco or llama, that useful compromise between the sheep and camel, and in winter it is easily captured in the deep snow. Two species of foxes, with a few small rodents of the mouse and bat families, and a very small number of birds found in the gloomy forests, complete the inland zoology of the region. But, as if to compensate for the want of life on land, the waters teem with colossal sea-weeds, so that Fuegia has been called the "paradise of fishes." These rugged coasts are the headquarters of those giants of the ocean Flora, the *Macrocystis* and *Lessonia*, the latter of which has a trunk like a tree, but, nevertheless, cannot be used as fuel, being as incombustible as stone. The *Macrocystis*, instead of having a trunk as thick as that of a cherry-tree, is moored to the rock by a tough but slender cable, and rising to the surface, breaks into leaves, and then streams along a luxuriant tangle for several hundred feet. These gigantic seaweeds are the home of countless molluscs and shoals of fishes, which, forsaking brighter waters, resort to them as to a well-stored larder; and in the wake of these fishes, come armies of seals and clouds of sea-fowl. Petrels, ducks, red-bills, penguins, etc., have their breeding-places on the cliffs of these islands. "O Lord, how manifold are thy works! in wisdom hast thou made them all: the earth is full of thy riches. So is this great and wide sea, wherein are things creeping innumerable, both small and great beasts. These wait all upon thee; that thou mayest give them their meat in due season."

The inhabitants of the Fuegian Archipelago are South American Indians, and belong to the Araucanian division of the great Andean race, a description of which we have already given in another part of our volume. They are, undoubtedly, of the closest kindred as well as near neighbours to the Patagonians, but they are intellectually and physically inferior to these stately specimens of mankind. Their colour is something between a dark copper and a brown, not unlike that of old mahogany, but owing to the wood-smoke with which they are saturated, the oil and blubber with which they are smeared, and the earths, white, red, and black, used in painting their faces, it is difficult to describe a Fuegian complexion. Their heads are large, their long black hair hangs down straight on either side, but is cropped away on the brow. The forehead is very low and broad, the black eyes are oval and usually expressive of good humour. The nose is flat and thick, with large nostrils, and the mouth is very wide and large. The men do not fancy long beards; and usually pull out what little hair shows itself on the chin and eyebrows, with tweezers made of two mussel-shells. Many of them have trunks proportionate to a six feet stature, but from constantly crouching in their huts and canoes their extremities are dwarfed and crooked; still they are by no means deficient in agility, and in trials of strength some can outmatch an English sailor. Their clothing is scanty. By the same providential arrangement, which coats the whale in the frozen seas with oil, the Fuegian is fortified against his inclement sky by an abundant develop-

BOUT ALIKHOOLI. FUEGIAN.

PATAGONIAN OF CAPE GREGORY.

Both drawn from Lithographs taken of the Originals in England
By Sarah A. Myers

T. Sinclair's lith Phil^a

ment of fat; by this underclothing of non-conducting fat any other garment than his cloak of sea-otter or guanaco skin is rendered unnecessary. In the coldest mid-winter, these islanders may be seen diving for sea-eggs, and are constantly exhibiting feats of hardihood, the bare recital of which makes a European shudder. Nothing can be more wretched than their habitations, which are always built by the women, who are the only workers. We have already described the arrangement of their huts, which are constructed with as much rapidity as a soldier pitches his tent. A fire is kindled in the middle, round which they huddle day and night in stormy weather, and they tarry in the same place till, having devoured all the food afforded by the district, they are forced to wander elsewhere. They love ornaments, and exhibit much ingenuity in making necklaces and bracelets from shells or bones; and jars or baskets have been found among them, entirely formed of bark, with the bottom so accurately sewed in, that they would contain water without leaking. Their canoes are, perhaps, a still more wonderful specimen of needlework, and are also made of bark. The main trunk may be the bark of a single beech; but in order to complete it, a great many patches and a large amount of stitching are requisite. With grass for oakum, clay for pitch, and thongs of hide instead of nails, the builder soon finishes a boat which, after its own fashion, is a triumph of naval architecture. Although their comforts are so few, they are well provided with offensive weapons, such as have been already described as being used by the Patagonians.

The inhabitants of the Fuegian Archipelago have by some been called Pesherais, from a word which they are constantly uttering; by others "the Ichthyophagi," or fish-eaters. They are, however, by no means expert fishers, and although the sea around them is teeming with food, it is but a scanty subsistence the Fuegian secures. He has neither net nor angle, and it is only when he is lucky enough to spear a rock salmon, or jerk the small fish out of the water with a baited but hookless line, that the "fish-eater" acquires his name. He is, however, a cunning bird-catcher, and trains his dogs to aid him in his fowling. But birds are not always to be procured, and even sea-eggs are not attainable in stormy weather; therefore, for a great period of the year, these poor islanders are entirely dependent on mussels, limpets, etc., and every time the tide retires, the whole population is seen spread over the shore, rummaging for this sorry subsistence. Sometimes they are so lucky as to discover a stranded whale or sea-lion; and no matter in what state the carcase may be, it is always welcome, and imparts a sudden plumpness to the finders. Of course such prizes are rare; and like most savages, the life of a Fuegian is an alternation of occasional feasts with long intervals of famine. In the desperation of hunger, it is fearful to think of the expedients to which these Indians are driven, for there is no doubt of their being cannibals, and not only do they feed upon the bodies of their enemies whom they vanquish in battle, but also kill and devour the old women of their own tribe, when other subsistence fails, before they sacrifice their dogs. Their powers of mimicry are amazing, and their memories remarkable, for they will repeat a long English sentence with the utmost precision: they are notorious thieves, and shamelessly greedy; and although traces of gentleness and tenderness are found among the women, the men are universally cruel, and when exasperated or brought to bay, they fight with more fury than wild beasts.*

They are very superstitious, and never speak of the dead. When Mr. Williams questioned a boy,

* An incident related by Commodore Byron shows the fearful wickedness which sometimes becomes universal among those to whom the softening influence of the domestic charities is scarcely known. "A cacique and his wife had gone off in their canoe, when she dived for sea-eggs; but not meeting with much success, they returned, much out of humour. A little boy of theirs, about three years, of whom they appeared to be doatingly fond, watching for his father and mother's return, ran into the surf to meet them. The father handed a basket of sea-eggs to the child, which being too heavy for him to carry, he let it fall; upon which the father jumped out of the canoe, and catching the boy up in his arms, dashed him with the utmost violence against the stones. The poor little creature lay motionless and bleeding, and in that condition was taken up by his mother; but died soon after. She appeared inconsolable for some time, but the brutish father showed little concern about it.

hereafter to be mentioned, about his dead father, he was very unhappy, and refused to answer: "No good talk; my country never talk of dead man."

In the year 1831 there were three Fuegians brought by Captain Fitzroy to England, and it was hoped that they would learn the language, and acquire some of the arts of civilization, so as to introduce them on their return to their countrymen. One of them was a full grown man, York Minster, a gruff and surly fellow, who could never be induced to learn anything. Jemmy Button was a boy of no great capacity, and Fuegia Basket was a rather pleasing and intelligent girl. Considerable interest was felt in these visitors from the antipodes, and King William IV. and Queen Adelaide expressing a desire to see them, they were taken to the palace, and received with all the gentle kindness characteristic of the queen. After passing a few months under the care of a schoolmaster, they, accompanied by a missionary, Mr. Matthews, were carried back by Captain Fitzroy to their native isles. It may be questioned whether their residence in England was sufficiently long; and it is likely that, had a selection been practicable, more promising pupils might have been found than York Minster and Jemmy Button. The experiment, however, proved very unproductive. On landing in their own country, York Minster married Fuegia Basket, and being a powerful, resolute man, it is possible that he may have been able to preserve from his rapacious neighbours the implements and manufactured articles with which he was freely supplied. But poor Jemmy was soon victimized. His little garden was trodden down; and his goods were stolen: justifying his verdict, "My people very bad: no sabe nothing: my people very great fool." And as the violence of the natives forced Mr. Matthews to return on board, there is too much reason to fear that, left to themselves, his scholars would soon relapse into the surrounding barbarism. Such then, as we have described, was the land and the people to whom the devoted little band we have been following, went, in order to teach them the words of life.

CHAPTER XVII.

FIRST TOILS.

"My wanderings thou hast numbered;
Even every tear mine eyes have shed
Thy vial holds,
All in the folds
Of thy large volume read."

On the 5th of December, the mission party proceeded in the ship's gig to a small island called Dothan, lying between Garden and Picton Islands, where Captain Gardiner proposed to fix the site of their intended dwelling-house. Here they read an appropriate psalm, and offered prayer, and sang the doxology. The natives had followed them, and while thus engaged, stood gazing with wonder. One of them passed into the circle, and now and then made an observation; but all joined heartily in the singing. On further consideration, however, they thought best to abandon Dothan, and choose a site in Garden Island, from which they cleared away the large timber. To this spot their bedding, cooking utensils, and stores were carried; and so great was their industry, that by nightfall their tents were erected, and their comfort pretty well secured. They had two tents—one for the men—and between the two, a kind of kitchen, made of poles which they had cut down and covered with oiled canvas. The floor of the tent was covered with cork, over which was spread oiled canvas, which made a dry place for their beds. They also began a fence around the tents, which on the next day was, by the aid of the ship's company, completed; each one plying the woodman's handicraft to the best of his power. Making a large fire, they gathered round it and regaled themselves with the provisions kindly sent from the ship by Captain Cooper. They had not been disturbed throughout the day by the natives, and congratulated themselves on this fortunate circumstance, as they hoped, by their not seeing their possessions, they would not be tempted to molest or steal from them. By eleven at night they had every thing so straight as to be able to retire to rest, which all did, except Captain Gardiner and Mr. Williams, who had agreed on keeping watch throughout the night. At the end of two hours they were to relieve each other. This the Captain proposed should be commenced by himself, taking the first watch at ten o'clock every night, and he now accordingly rigged in his india-rubber overcoat and sou-wester, for the rain was pouring down with Fuegian earnestness. At half-past twelve he was relieved by Mr. Williams. The latter had not lain down, on account of the shortness of the time before commencing his watch; and now while he was alone in the dead hours of the night, surrounded by the dark masses of the wood on the one hand, and the rippling waters on the other, with the rain pouring down in heavy showers, his heart was oppressed with a heaviness for which he could not account. He says, "The time of my watch hung heavily upon me, and I almost counted the minutes as they passed. Strange cries broke upon my ear: the penguin's harsh croak, with the shrill whistle of some sea-bird, and many sounds for which I could scarce account, all tending to give an extraordinary character to the scene. I felt no fear, neither did I wish to be differently circumstanced; but I was weary, and longed for rest. Two o'clock came, and then was Mr. Maidment's turn. Selfish nature was glad of the opportunity to exchange positions even thus with a friend and brother, and comforting myself in the warmth and repose of bed, I slept soundly, and awoke the next morning, ready to resume the labours of the day." They persevered all Saturday in completing their fence, and arranging matters to their satisfaction, without being molested by any of the natives; a matter at which they would have been surprised, had they not conjectured that they were going to give to others of the tribe, the intelligence of the stranger's arrival.

In the evening, however, three whom they had seen before came up. Without evincing any surprise, they greeted the strangers with apparent good-nature, *yammer-schoonering* after everything they saw, and trying to peep inside the enclosure; but on Captain Gardiner intimating his disapproval, they were very tractable. Altogether they seemed so peaceable and well-disposed, that our pioneers had good hope of being able to maintain a friendly intercourse with them. Toward evening, Captain Gardiner made signs for them to leave, intimating that it was time to go to sleep, by laying his head on his hand, and then gently directing them to the entrance. They readily comprehended the meaning, and without hesitation departed. On Sunday, however, just as the morning service was commenced, the same party came again, but remained very quietly near the tent door, little thinking how nearly they themselves stood concerned in what was going on. Nothing occurred to break the sacred stillness of the Sabbath, until late in the afternoon, when our pioneers were startled by the mournful yelling of some of the women from their canoes, which sounded like the prolonged howl of a dog. The Fuegians, who still were in the tent, pricked up their ears, and taking up their spears, immediately departed in haste, making signs that the strangers were not to follow. They took the road leading to Banner Cove; which having reached, they were seen, by the help of glasses, to be joined by another party.

In the course of a few hours the new-comers appeared, who, as was easily seen, belonged to another tribe. Their faces were quite blackened over; they were impudent and uncontrollable, and unlike the former, they were ready to resent every refusal of their unreasonable demands. Their whole demeanor plainly bespoke intended mischief: nevertheless, they were very well made, and, but for the diabolical passions expressed in their countenances, were good-looking men. With five of such men around them, prying into everything, the other three having also assumed a less pacific deportment, and almost entering the tent by force, the situation of our friends was by no means agreeable. It required all their vigilance to watch their motions; and from their whispering together, it was suspected that they were concocting some plan of attack. Captain Gardiner, however, after a time succeeded in sending them off, and the Sunday evening service being over, the watch was set, and the party retired to bed. A railway whistle, which had been provided to be used as an alarm, raised its shrill warning near four o'clock in the morning, and startled the sleepers, who were up and dressed in an instant. The disturbance was caused by the coming of the two black-faced natives, who, determined on intruding, gave sufficient cause for uneasiness, and behaved with such audacity to Mr. Maidment and Bryant, pushing one off his seat, and endeavouring to pull off the other's boots, that forcible resistance became necessary. After remaining two hours, they grew tired and left, but in the course of the morning returned with an augmented party, and again visited the tents. So determined was their conduct, almost bordering on open hostility, that it became manifest the mission party could no longer stay on shore; therefore Captain Gardiner resolved that, with the aid of the men from the *Ocean Queen*, he would at once strike the tents, and have all their stores carried on board the boats. This was his original intention, but he was anxious, whilst Captain Cooper's vessel remained, to try an establishment on land, so as to see what disposition the natives would evince. All were glad when he announced his determination to abandon the land, for most were convinced that to stay another night on shore would be attended with the loss of property, and perhaps of life. On Monday evening, therefore, all their effects were transported on board the *Ocean Queen*, where they remained until their boats were ready.

Notwithstanding their horizon was now so dark with portentous clouds, and they were fully sensible what dangers, difficulties, and privations awaited them on all hands, not one of this devoted party regretted the step they had taken. If any one will be the disciple of Christ, he must be willing to leave all and follow him; and now this little band of pioneers, leaving the lap of comfort to travel the thorny path of what they believed duty, were not without their reward. Given up to the service of the Saviour, they lived in the enjoyment of his love.

"His consolations and the comforts of the Holy Ghost," says Williams, "are infinitely precious and outweigh all privations we have to encounter." Going out on a sailing excursion with Captain Cooper, Mr. Williams took one of the Fuegians in the boat, and in order to try what impression could be made on his mind by firing a gun, shot a penguin. The sight of the wounded bird occasioned much more interest and curiosity than did the gun, although he evinced some little fear of the latter, and did not like it to be brought near him. They took this man on board, and rigged him out in some clothes given by the sailors, and afterwards carried him back with them to their station. They gave him the bird, which, when some of his companions joined him, he put on the burning embers, singed the feathers, then plucked them off, and having laid it on the fire again for a quarter of an hour, it was ready cooked according to their taste; and then, borrowing a knife from one of the men, which he afterwards returned, he dissected it, giving each one of the party a portion. These again bit off pieces and gave them to each other. And thus they devoured the whole fowl with a voracity truly frightful, leaving no part except the bones and feathers.

The *Ocean Queen* left them on the 19th December, bearing letters to England written in the most hopeful spirit, and such cheerful communications were well calculated to remove any inquietude or anxiety from the minds of their anxious friends at home. They knew that the stores, the missionary pioneers had taken with them, were sufficient to last till June, that they had also guns and abundance of ammunition, besides nets for fishing. They knew also, that Gardiner had made arrangements with Mr. Lafone, of Monte Video; that a vessel should ply periodically between the Falkland Islands and Fuego, bringing provisions for the mission, and carrying back wood; and believed that the mission-boats could retreat to the colony, in case of necessity. But as time passed, and no further intelligence was heard, application was made to the Admiralty for assistance, which was promptly rendered. Captain Morshead, of H. M. S. *Dido* received directions to touch at Picton Island, on his way to the Pacific, and left England in October, 1851.

The *Ocean Queen* was hardly out of sight, when Gardiner, according to a plan before named, prepared for a voyage to Button Island, and on the same day commenced to search for a safe place to deposit the stores, whilst they repaired the *Pioneer*, which had sprung a leak. In this insecure vessel, Gardiner led the way, taking with him Mr. Maidment, Pearce, and Bryant. The two dingeys were towed behind the *Pioneer*. Then followed the *Speedwell*, laden with the spare timber, with Mr. Williams, Erwin, and Badcock on board. Bravely the *Pioneer* struggled with the heavy sea, but at length reached a safe inlet, which Gardiner named Blomefield Harbour; but just before entering the harbour, both the dingeys were carried away. Here they waited for many hours in great anxiety for their companions. At four o'clock on the following day they put to sea in search for them, and on coming in sight of their old anchorage, they gladly descried the form of the *Speedwell*, just descernible in the darkness. They shouted, but received no answer. "All was still," says Gardiner, "not a sound was heard, but the plashing of the oars, and the murmurs of the surf on the beach. It was an awful suspense, not a word was uttered among us. We were now actually alongside, but no movement or sound was heard on board. I confess my blood ran cold." The three fearless men, of whom they were in search, were, meantime, sleeping in the cabin of the *Speedwell* as soundly as if on their native shores. It was three in the morning when they were aroused by the shouts of their companions. Mr. Williams explained that the raft which the *Speedwell* was towing had caught in a mass of kelp, and, in consequence, the greatest exertion had been necessary to keep the vessel from drifting on the surf. The danger was avoided, but the anchor and timber were lost, and they were only able to return to Banner Cove. Thus the first day's expedition resulted in the loss of the *Speedwell's* anchor, the timber, and both of the dingeys. The last, especially, was a very serious loss. A second attempt was, therefore, made to reach Blomefield Harbour. The *Speedwell* and *Pioneer* remained in company for several hours;

but in the course of the day, the *Speedwell* gradually distanced her consort; and the *Pioneer*, being becalmed under the land, returned to Picton Island. Having no landing boat, they were obliged to anchor very near the beach, and our four friends retired to rest after the fatigues of the day. They were aroused in the morning by the shouting of the natives, and on reaching the deck they were alarmed to find that the boat was immovable, the tide having left her aground. There were no signs of the *Speedwell*, and it was difficult to keep off the rough handling of the natives. As the Fuegians increased in number, and seemed bent on boarding the *Pioneer*, Gardiner and his companions landed, armed with guns, and walked towards them. With their arms in their hands they knelt down, and implored the protection of that Saviour whose servants they were, being determined not to use any violence towards men whom they came to befriend, except as a last necessity. When the Fuegians saw their visitors in prayer they seemed awe-struck. A few presents were made, but any further friendly intercourse, without the knowledge of a common language, was impossible. While this was going forward, the *Speedwell* arrived, and the *Pioneer* soon getting afloat, both boats returned to Banner Cove.

It was now apparent that, short-handed as they were for the management of two boats in so stormy a channel, they must lighten them before attempting to find a safe harbour in which to re-fit for a voyage to Woollya or Button Island. They therefore stowed away part of their provisions under ground, at Banner Cove, where they were. In unloading the *Speedwell* for this purpose, they were shocked at the discovery, that the powder which they had brought with them in the *Ocean Queen* had never been landed. One flask and a-half was all they had now, and thus early were they deprived of an important means of obtaining fresh food. Startled, but not dispirited, they carefully concealed part of their precious store, and endeavoured to stop the leak in the *Pioneer* and to enter into a friendly barter with the natives. They were not able to stay long, for the natives, being provided with canoes in which baskets of stones and war-spears were observed, were evidently meditating an attack. The boats, therefore, once more made sail for Lennox Island; but so varying were the winds, so continual the sudden squalls, that the passage to Lennox Island lasted twenty-seven hours.

Whilst at Tent Cove they were again alarmed by a party of natives. The alarm whistle was blown at four o'clock in the morning, and all hands were immediately on deck, in order to be prepared in case of an attack. The party consisted of eight men with their families in three canoes; but, although they came alongside, they showed no actually hostile spirit, as our friends feared they would; because on the night previous they had hung up white streamers on their canoes and painted themselves white, which they knew meant hostility. But as Captain Gardiner gave them no presents on this occasion, but rather intimated dissatisfaction with them, they soon left the bay; and the pioneer band at once availed themselves of the opportunity to get back the raft of timber which was lying on the beach opposite their wigwams; and they also succeeded in recovering some other property of importance.

They spent Christmas day at Banner Cove, but it was a day of bustle and work, as they overhauled the *Pioneer* to get at the leak. Their Christmas-dinner consisted of preserved meat, and some wheat-meal dough with a few raisins in it; and as they enjoyed this plain repast, spread out in this, the most remote, portion of the earth, they remembered their dear friends at home, and in God's name blessed them.

The natives returned, but in a friendly manner, and having bartered some small fish which they had speared, passed on quietly to their wigwams. The want of the powder left on board the *Ocean Queen* was a great disappointment; for, although there were plenty of ducks and geese, they had no means of killing them; and another, not less, was the expectation of finding fish, of which there were scarcely any; but, appalled as they must have been at the great difficulties which surrounded them, no signs of discontent were exhibited, and the most affectionate intercourse subsisted among them. As they had not anticipated either of these failures, no large provision of animal food was made; they had now only two casks of preserved meat, and one of pork; therefore they lived principally on wheat and oat meal, with rice, biscuit, cheese, butter, and molasses. Speaking of these trials, Mr. Williams says, "Every circumstance that has occurred in this land of storms has tended to the same end—to humble and abase me. The privation of accustomed comforts, the vicissitudes already experienced, the trying duties devolving on us, the dulness and great inclemency of the climate, the solitude of the scenery, the uninviting character of the natives, and the apparent hopelessness of contending with so many difficulties,—all these things the flesh has had to be loaded with, and, together with its own fears and repinings, to be nailed to the cross, and yield up the ghost, whilst in the room thereof Christ should be raised up and formed in me the hope of glory."

CHAPTER XVIII.

NEW TRIALS.

"Lord, listen to my lowly dirge,
  My plaintive call attend;
My fainting heart to thee would urge
  A prayer from earth's far end.

Within thy tabernacle's shade
  I would for aye abide,
In wings of thy kind sheltering aid
  Would safely rest and hide."

HAD the funds of the mission admitted of the purchase of a vessel of a hundred tons burden, the mission party would have been comparatively independent. If it became dangerous to remain on shore, they would have found secure refuge on shipboard, and when provisions failed, they could have procured a supply by going to Port Famine or the Falklands. In that case they would also have been spared the fatigue and anxiety of hiding their stores where there was great risk of the natives finding them, and instead of creeping around these dreary coasts in boats too small to weather a storm, and in which they could scarcely secure a dry berth, they would at least have lodged in comfort and faced the blast with some confidence. But in their shallop launches, they were as much imprisoned in the Fuegian island as was Alexander Selkirk in Juan Fernandez; and to reach a Christian settlement across such turbulent seas, would have been little less than a miracle. But Gardiner, although he knew that the chances of European vessels visiting their rendezvous were very small, believed he should be able to surmount every difficulty. He knew that there were fish in the sea, and abundance of birds on the shore. He had provisions for six months; and before these could be exhausted he calculated on fresh supplies from England. And, although none knew better the wildness of these waters, he trusted, should it be found impossible to propitiate the natives, to find a retreat where the little party might hold out until succours arrived. We have seen, however, how these calculations were disappointed. The low-decked boats, whose iron roofs condensed the vapor and kept a continual rain dripping on the berths and floors, were rendered partly unserviceable from the loss of the two "dingeys," which were intended as a communication between the launches and the land. We have already mentioned the fearful oversight by which the powder was left in the ship, and although, therefore, there were fowling-pieccs and good marksmen in the party, they had less power to secure the game with which they were surrounded, than the savages who had nothing but slings. The net they had brought with them, they were also destined to lose; so that in a climate beyond all others requiring warm shelter and generous diet, these devoted men soon found themselves without cordials, without animal food or dry clothing; in short, without a single material comfort. But we will resume our narrative, which we take from the journal of Mr. Williams.

At Tent Cove the missionaries were, as we have already mentioned, if not alarmed, at least rendered suspicious by the behaviour of the natives, who mustered together at an early hour, giving strong indications of having a hostile purpose. From the singular behaviour of these people, it was evident that the Fuegians were not to be trusted, and that now their cupidity was greatly excited by the sight of the mission property. They were perfect in the art of dissimulation. When the missionary party were few in number and the ship remained, they were quiet enough; but as soon as these circumstances changed, they became insolent and unruly. The boldness and troublesome conduct of the party who disturbed our missionaries at Garden Island, has already been mentioned, and repeatedly since then there had been occasion to notice the haughtiness of their bearing. One of them, one day, entered Captain Gardiner's tent where he was writing, and laying his heavy hand on the inkstand, poured the whole contents on the unfinished page. But the most forward and insolent of all, was an individual whom, for the sake of distinction, they named "Jemmy." This man, who acted in some measure as chief, was well formed and well featured, and possessed an unusual energy and quickness of mind, was the ring-leader in all the evil. He invariably rejected all articles of a trifling character with contempt, and the withering smile which passed across his lips when such were offered, showed that he considered the strangers of no importance. They had also some suspicions of "Jemmy," which caused them great uneasiness. They had found in a certain place the mutilated and charred remains of a human body, the skin of the head and face being undestroyed; and they were not without a strong suspicion that he had been the perpetrator of this act of malevolence. A sling was found near these remains. Another thing they noticed in "Jemmy," was his frequent change of complexion. At first he and his companions were painted black, this was afterwards exchanged for white streaks; and this in turn gave place to another painting of white dots, regularly arranged. The only redeeming trait he possessed was his seeming kindness to his two wives, and whatever beads or light articles our friends gave him, he immediately handed over to them.

The mission party remained some days in Lennox Cove without being molested; but on Saturday morning, January 4th, the signal was given by the look-out that the natives were approaching, and indeed "Jemmy" and some others of their old acquaintance were soon alongside. Eight canoes were coming in sight, and as there are usually two men and sometimes more in each canoe, our friends knew that they were greatly superior to them in strength. Captain Gardiner got his glass, and plainly saw that they were come prepared to attack the boats. They were well provided with war spears; and moreover, they were taking in stones from the beach, the most certain evidence of their warlike intentions. No time was now to be lost, and with all speed both boats were got under sail. The merciful Providence of God was made manifest in what the party had considered disappointments. Had they been lying in Tent Cove, as had been proposed the day before, they never should have got out of it in time. Had the tents been rigged, as they had been until two days before, when the high winds compelled that they should be taken down, they would not have been able to get the boats ready soon enough. And, lastly, had not a breeze sprung up just at the very minute it was needed, they could not have sailed out as they did, and prevented an attack before the enemy had time to enclose them. The marks of disappointment and chagrin were plainly evident in the manner of the natives when they saw their intended victims safely passing beyond their reach. But although they escaped with their lives unharmed, it was not without much inconvenience to themselves and injury to their property. In their sudden flight they had to cut away the raft they had built as a substitute for the dingeys, as well as the hawser by which they were moored. They were also unprovided with water and wood; and the boats, not being properly rigged, could not put out to sea. They therefore shaped their course to Picton Island, hoping to find a cove on the south side, but in vain; about noon a dead calm came on, and they lay for some time anchored to the kelp. Here Captain Gardiner offered up a prayer to God, in gratitude for their merciful deliverance. "Whilst we were lying here," says Mr. Williams, "the Captain expressed himself as being now entirely left to the directing hand of God, and that nothing remained for us, but to leave it to his good providence to direct us where next we should go. Indeed, nothing that we had devised had issued in success, and we seemed to be getting disastrously crippled; being now without means of getting ashore, unless unusual facilities should be afforded in the character of the harbour." Although Navarin island had the disadvantage of being peopled thickly with the natives, they resolved, as the wind was in their favour, to go thither; but a breeze sprang up in the night, which soon increased to a heavy gale, and with wind and tide against them, they were unable to beat through the channel, and bore up for Lennox Island, where they arrived on Sunday morning, January 5th. The *Pioneer*, just as they were running in on the beach, was taken aback by the wind and driven among a reef of rocks, and escaped destruction as by a miracle.

There was nothing very inviting in the appearance of Lennox Harbour or the island; but a resting place from storms, where our weary travellers could be some time undisturbed by the natives and complete their boats, was very desirable, and they felt truly thankful when they saw neither wigwam nor natives in the harbour. On the day after their arrival, it was found that they could not get the boat afloat, the tide on the previous morning being higher than usual, owing to the force of the tempest. They would therefore have to wait for the next spring-tide, some nine or ten days; and if the natives should come, they must fall an easy prey, for they would have no means to escape. But in these distressing circumstances, instead of giving way to apprehensions, they only more and more leaned on that faith which makes the Christian forgetful of every temporal evil. The position of our pioneers in this antarctic Patmos was now very critical; and to make the peril more imminent, two of their number returned from a walk, with the tidings that there were natives in the adjoining coves. Although no position could present more occasion for fear and anxiety, "not one of the party gave indication that either was felt; all solicitude was hushed into repose by our hope in God." There was but one member of the party who did not profess to have experienced a renewing change, and he was now becoming "a brother in the kingdom and patience of Jesus Christ." On the same day they were unpleasantly surprised by the sight of two fine Fuegian dogs, a sure indication that their masters were not far off. However, although the dogs were again seen, no natives appeared. In the neighbouring cove there was a wigwam, and an enormous pile of mussel-shells, and here too, they found human remains—a skull and bones of the extremities. They also saw a canoe approaching the cove, and smoke issuing from the wigwam; but on the next day they left, without discovering the ships and our mission party.

After waiting patiently for the moon to enlargo her borders and approach to the full; after digging away the sand from under the *Speedwell*, at an immense expense of labour; after hope as to the practicability of getting off at all grew less and less, our readers may imagine with what joy each one heard the words shouted, "She is afloat!" Little time was spent after this announcement in the exposed shelter of Lennox Harbour, and as Captain Gardiner in a walk across the country a few days before, had found a cove, which, seeming to promise safety, he had named Mercy Cove, they now directed their course thither.

The last few days of their stay at Lennox Island had been marked by visits from a party of the natives, seemingly one family. They were very quiet and docile, and one of the men very good-looking, with a pleasing expression of countenance. It seemed uncharitable to think evil of him, or suspect he meditated harm. As they saw no other party, our friends were quite easy whilst they continued with them, but were afraid they might go off for others. They did leave and return more than once, and were absent at the time when they left Lennox Harbour.

As we have stated, they shaped their course for Mercy Cove, and after surmounting many difficulties, when abreast of a cluster of islands, they saw a large body of natives on the beach, among whom was their late acquaintance of Lennox Island. They were engaged in fishing or hunting seals, which were very plentiful at that place. They no sooner caught sight of our friends than, as usual, the uproar was great; canoes were immediately put off and paddled with a speed almost incredible. Our pioneers were now within a short distance of Mercy Cove; but it was evident that, if they proceeded, the whole party of about five and twenty persons would follow; and not wishing to be at their mercy, Captain Gardiner regretfully turned back upon his path, and anchored once more in Lennox Harbour. Although next morning was Sunday, the Captain thought it advisable to get under weigh again, with the intention of going to Cape Rees, or Blomefield Harbour, where he hoped they could spend the Sabbath in quiet. The wind at first was light and favourable, and the morning promising; but the breeze soon freshened into a gale, the bowsprit of the *Speedwell* was carried away, and she was also otherwise injured. It was a time of great danger, and they were obliged once more to seek refuge in Lennox Harbour. As they entered the mouth of the harbour, they had to make great exertions to keep off the rocks. The wind now blew a hurricane; the anchor dragged, and they were threatened with destruction. They were smitten throughout the whole day by the pitiless blasts; the dark foaming water raged around them; the dark clouds poured down their pelting hailstones and deluges of rain. "Nothing could be more fearful," says Mr. Williams in his journal; "we were anything but sheltered, being near the entrance of the harbour, and within thirty feet of the rocks, against which had we dashed, we must inevitably have been lost. But God in his providential mercy was with us. We all felt we had done wrong in getting under weigh on Sunday morning, and greatly did I feel relieved when I heard the Captain say, that he also felt it wrong. 'Never,' said he, 'never have I commenced a journey on the Sabbath before, and this shall be the last time.'"

On Monday following, January 20th, the day being fine, they again sailed for Blomefield Harbour, off which they arrived at half-past eight o'clock. As they got in sight of the harbour, they saw several fires, and were soon apprised that there was a good party of the natives present. Three canoes put off, and it being calm at the time, they soon came up. Among them was one of their Banner Cove acquaintances, and a member of the hostile league organized against them there. Their errand was now useless. No rest nor quiet was now to be expected here, and it was certain that the natives would soon accumulate an overwhelming force, and overpower their small and feeble party. Once more they were obliged to turn back upon their route, and seek a temporary asylum at Banner Cove. They kept under sail all night, it being for the most part of the time a calm. Near Picton Island a canoe put off, in which they recognized the intimate associate of Jemmy, the great concerter of all the attacks made upon them, and their most troublesome acquaintance. Banner Roads would now be no shelter for them; the hue and cry would go forth, and it was certain that they would at once be surrounded. Thus being driven out of every asylum, and from the crippled state of their boats being quite impracticable to beat about from place to place, an opportunity was sought to confer together as to the course proper to be pursued in the midst of such perplexities. The Captain offered up prayer —a prayer breathed in godly sincerity, and in firm reliance upon the goodness and providential direction of a Heavenly Father; and afterwards it was decided that an eastward course should be pursued, and if a convenient cove could not be found, they would proceed to Spaniard Harbour.

Once more they set forth in search of an asylum, and found a cove where they might make a short stay and take in water and wood. In the course of their walk over the headland, which, going and returning, occupied five hours, they saw a guanaco acting as a scout, perched on the highest point of land, and watching the party with close scrutiny. Before they got very near, with a leap and bound in the air, it gave the signal to the herd and started off. They saw the foot-prints of these animals very numerous, and also many Indian paths; the only other traces of natives was a wigwam on the beach.

The next day our devoted party reached Spaniard Harbour, where they hoped to have got to a place of refuge, and, for a time at least, to have rest from their wanderings. They remembered their long and troublesome passage in the *Ocean Queen* over the same ground they had now traversed so pleasantly and easily, and seeing the hand of God in his mercy and favouring providence, unitedly gave to him the praise and the glory. It was now the twenty-fifth of January, and the sun shining out quite warm, the delightful weather had a most invigorating effect upon the missionary party. In some places the scenery was quite pleasing. Spots of good meadow-land, valleys, and copses of wood, with a bold range of mountains and hilly bluffs, met the eye in its furthest range. Even Terra del

Fuego could put on a pleasing aspect, and throw around a radiance which communicated itself to the spirits. Why should not the benighted children of Fuegia be recovered from the darkness that surrounded them? There were smiling spots of nature here, which cultivation might reclaim from wildness, and where Christian men could live; and why, then, should Fuegia alone of all the earth be left without the gospel light? So thought the meek and pious Williams, as he explored the as yet untrodden ground, forcing his way through the almost impervious copses of a species of currant-bush. On returning to the boats, he found them on the opposite bank, and, as the tide was ebbing, they were both aground. As they had, therefore, no means of sending for him, he was obliged to walk and find a fordable place for crossing the stream. In order to accomplish this, he penetrated farther inland, and found the country more open and the trees larger, but perceiving a few wigwams at no great distance, he deemed a retreat prudent, as he was now some miles away from the boats. He therefore crossed the river where he was, and after a long journey, now in the forest and now in the plain, he found, but not without some difficulty, his way back again, hungry and fatigued, after having been absent five or six hours.

They remained at Cook's river until January 28, when finding it very inconvenient to get on shore, as well as imprudent to be so long aground, they removed to a well-sheltered inlet called Earnest Cove. Until this time they had been cheered with the prevalence of fine weather, some of the days, for a short time, equalling in warmth and brightness a summer's day in England. At nightfall, however, it usually became cold, though sometimes there were exceptions, the temperature remaining high and even close. On Friday, the last day of January, after a beautiful day, the weather began to look squally and to rain heavily, and continued to do so all night. A heavy gale was blowing in the offing, but the boats rode very snugly, protected from the wind which blew off the shore. The swell of the sea caused a great strain on the hawsers, the jerks of which, felt by all, kept them awake during the night. The impression made upon the minds of most of them was a vivid suggestion of danger; but none gave way to despondence or fear. Mr. Williams declares, "a very heaven of repose and love was around me, and my heart rested so assuredly and implicitly in God, that it was blissful to feel as I did. Awakened repeatedly by the jerk of the hawsers, and the strain of the boats, and hearing the roar and dash of the water around, the pelting of the rain and hail, and the howl of the sweeping blasts, something would point to danger as present; but I quietly resigned myself to slumber, after communion with the Keeper of Israel, whose eye I knew was over me. In the morning, I heard the Captain give orders for the *Speedwell* to cast off from her stern, apprehensive, it seemed, of the hawser giving way, as both boats were riding by it. Scarce a minute elapsed after this was done before the concussion of the boat against the beach was felt, and almost as instantly a swell broke over her stern and into our dormitory. I could scarcely credit my senses. Another and another thump, and another sea breaking in over us, confirmed me in the fact that something fearful had happened. On looking out, I found the Captain and Pearce were busily occupied with poles, and endeavouring to keep her broadside from the surf; but this seemed next to impossible, as the water was pouring into the after part of the boat, tumbling right over the stern-sheets, and threatening to float everything. The poor *Pioneer* was evidently upon the rocks. Owing to the force of the swell, no effort could keep her from swinging on them, and she rolled backwards and forwards upon the surge, threatening to knock herself to pieces. It was useless to bail any longer, and we soon gave up all hope of doing anything for her, but proceeded as rapidly as we could to get our things out of her. Our Captain, always first in everything, now got into the cabin to hand out the things, and by this time our boxes were already floating, and the most of our goods wet. Mr. Maidment and I waded through the surf and the swell, backwards and forwards, carrying ashore the bedding and tools as the Captain and Pearce handed them out."

At nightfall, a storm of snow came on, and some of the party took refuge in a large cavern, which opened to the sea, and was quite near to where the boat had stranded. They found shells cast up at the further end of the cavern, which made it evident that under extraordinary tides with gales of wind concurring, the water reached so far,—no agreeable information to those who proposed taking up their night's quarters there. But as there was no cause for present apprehension, they lighted a fire near the entrance of the cave, and after refreshment and prayer, committed themselves to God as unto a faithful Creator. In spite of wet clothes and strong apprehensions, they got a sound night's rest. The roar of the water as it washed through the archway of a huge rock, met with another army of waves from the opposite side, and then, in a mighty struggle against each other, heaving and foaming, came bellowing into the cave. "This roar of water," says Mr. Williams, "disturbed me now and then, and the thought that, like some voracious animal, it was almost upon us, just occurred to me; but it could not drive away sleep from my eyes, for I was at peace with God, and had hope in him."

Captain Gardiner at first entertained hopes that the *Pioneer* might be repaired, and that her damages were not very serious. But it was found that her bows were driven in by the jagged root of a large tree which lay prostrate on the beach, and her bilge so much injured that nothing could be done to save her. The weather continuing stormy, hail, rain, and snow succeeding each other, the wind blowing a gale and the sea foaming, the work of destruction was completed. The party were entirely confined to the cave, which proved to be very damp, and the smoke of the fire drifting into it, made it no agreeable residence; although, in their emergency, they felt it to be a mercifully provided shelter. They had, in all this trouble, no opportunity of communicating with the *Speedwell*, but on Monday, Feb. 2, the weather had subsided sufficiently for the crew to come ashore on the raft; they, too, had been in danger, and were obliged to take their stove and attach it to a hawser, and throw it out as an anchor; in case her chain cable parted, therefore they could not cook anything. They continued their residence in the cavern for several days, during which time they employed themselves in hauling the remains of the *Pioneer* higher on the beach, and with the help of the tent and some oiled canvas, they converted it into a comfortable sleeping-place. It might now have been possible, had the weather been mild, to proceed to Woollya in the *Speedwell*, with seven hands on board, five of whom were men bred to the sea, taking with them part of their provisions; but having lost their landing boats in one gale and the *Pioneer* itself in another, they felt it would be useless to make any further attempt with their present means. They determined, therefore, to wait in Spaniard Harbour till the arrival of the relieving vessel from England or the Falklands, which they had reason to expect about the commencement of April. The possibility of a vessel not arriving did not occur to one of the party. The result of their consultation is given by Mr. Williams. "How evident," says he, "that we were not in a position to commence, with such slight means, so arduous an undertaking! But all this is well; the mission has thereby begun, which, had we awaited for more efficient means, it probably never would have been. We are all agreed that nothing short of a brigantine or schooner of eighty or a hundred tons burden can answer our ends, and to procure this ultimately, the Captain has fully determined to use every effort. Our plan of action is now to 'rough it' through all the circumstances it shall please God to permit to happen to us, until the arrival of a vessel, and then to take some Fuegians, and go to the Falkland Islands, there to learn their language, and when we have acquired it, and got the necessary vessel, to come out again, and go amongst them."

CHAPTER XIX.

SICKNESS AND FAMINE.

"Though round me the waves of adversity roll,
Though rocks of destruction encompass my soul,
In vain this frail vessel the tempest shall toss,
My hope rests secure on the blood of the cross."

It soon became impossible to alter the decision mentioned in the preceding chapter, for the humidity of the climate and continual hardships began to tell on the health of the party. The first sufferer was the young surgeon, Mr. Williams; his disorder began with a violent cold, but early in March symptoms of scurvy were apparent. John Badcock was the next, who showed signs of the same disease. In order to make more room for the invalids, Captain Gardiner made a little shelter for himself under a projecting rock, with poles and canvas. Cold and cheerless as this place was, he seems to have enjoyed it for a few days, and called it "the Hermitage." But it was soon destroyed by the fire, which had been ineffectual to keep it warm. To obviate the possibility of a relieving vessel missing them, they seized the opportunity, when Mr. Williams recovered from the violence of his first attack, to proceed once more to Banner Cove. They had a double object in doing so; to leave directions to any vessel to look for them in Spaniard Harbour, and to bring away their remaining provisions from the place of concealment. All day they were tossed by the waves, but steadily made way; at night a heavy swell arose, and the sea broke over the deck. Not wishing to expose Mr. Williams to the fatigue of a longer passage, they anchored early in the morning in a harbour, which they called Reliance Cove. Here they remained for three days. Although Mr. Williams was unable to leave his bed, and was much distressed with pains in his limbs and debility; although he felt that his disease was gaining ground every day, he availed himself of every opportunity to teach and encourage his companions. The Captain and Mr. Maidment took a long walk to explore the coast in the direction of Banner Cove, to find, if possible, a better anchorage. Mr. Williams says in his journal, "They will have a terrible walk; for the Captain is iron-hearted as to difficulties, and almost incapable of fatigue; he will yield to nothing but impossibilities, but Mr. Maidment is too weak and unwell for such a trial of strength. In their absence I have had the men together, and joined with them in a hymn and prayer. It was like a little heaven below. Thank God, the Captain and Mr. Maidment returned in safety, coming back a little after nine o'clock, having gone more than sixteen miles through a rough and mountainous country. Much to my surprise, Mr. Maidment seems less affected than the Captain, who, for the first time, has expressed himself fatigued."

On Saturday, March 21st, they left Reliance Harbour to seek some new abode. Whither they were bound, circumstances would decide. They named the place Reliance Cove, not on account of the protection it was capable of affording, but because of their reliance upon God, who made it a place of shelter by the way. Both nights of their stay there had been stormy, and the wind threatened to blow hard, which, had it done, their boat would have been dashed in pieces on the sharp shingle beach. Mr. Williams deemed their putting in to that cove as an especial providence; had they proceeded to Banner Cove, they must have been lost. Trusting themselves and their cockle-shell of a boat once more to the treacherous sea, attended by boisterous squalls, "williwaws" with hail and snow, and every moment in danger of their frail vessel with its disproportioned deck-load capsizing, they reached Banner Cove. Mr. Williams wrote in his journal at this time, "I am much affected by the kindness of the Captain, and his humble and gentle deportment. His prayer yesterday was an outpouring of his soul before God, in so unaffected and sincere a manner, with such unqualified expressions of resignation to the will, and humble trust in the mercy of God, that it made me own with joy, that here was a child of God addressing the Father of all mercies." Arriving near their old station, on looking in the direction of their old quarters, they discovered a light from a fire, kindled, as they thought, in their wigwam. They concluded that it had been taken possession of by the natives, but this was not the case. In the morning it was discovered a new wigwam had been built near it, and they soon had ocular demonstration that a large party of natives was established there. Every heart was now heavy with the expectation of a repetition of their former trials. Every moment they were sure they would behold the face of the redoubtable Jemmy and his associates, their late mortal foes. But they were agreeably surprised to find that the party, numbering fifteen, were entire strangers, and much more gentle in their bearing. On Monday, they began to recover the provisions which they had stowed away, including a barrel of pork and three barrels of biscuits. The goats they had left on Garden Island, they were sorry to discover, were all gone. Their next business was to bury some bottles with notes in them, containing the following directions: "We have gone to Spaniard Harbour which is on the main island, not far from Cape Kinnaird. We have sickness on board: our supplies are nearly out, and, if not soon relieved, we shall be starved. The natives are hostile." Having buried these notes, and fixed white stakes in the ground, marked with black crosses, and proper directions, Captain Gardiner painted on the rocks in one place, "Gone to Spaniard Harbour," and in another, "You will find us in Spaniard Harbour." Before these notices were finished, a fresh party of natives made their appearance, among whom were some of their old and evil-disposed acquaintances. They were very boisterous and presuming, and cut the rope attached to the raft, which with great difficulty was recovered from going adrift. Our seven friends now left Banner Cove for the last time, and sailed for Spaniard Harbour, "the only place where they hoped to find rest for the soles of their feet;" and where they proposed to remain until a vessel came to their relief. In these distressing circumstances, with sickness among them, and threatened with constant danger of all kinds, no murmurings were heard among them. They knew that the broad eye of God was resting upon them, and that, although seemingly dead to their friends and the busy world, they were "living in God and to God." They set sail at an early hour in the morning; every movement on the part of the natives convincing them that a large reinforcement was expected in the course of the day. No hindrance however was opposed to their leaving, and aided by a favouring wind, they reached Earnest Cove in safety on the afternoon of the next day. Here they enjoyed the blessing of rest, but as they had not suitable food, sickness progressed, not rapidly, but surely. Mr.

Williams and John Badcock were the greatest sufferers, and soon became unable to go forth at all. The boat in which they had their berths was very unsuitable to their condition. If the entrance door to the berths was shut, all air for ventilation was excluded; if it was open, they were half frozen. The vapour from their breaths accumulated on the iron roof of the deck, which was only a few inches higher than their pillows, and dropped and trickled down in such quantities that it was very troublesome. The preserved meat was fast hastening to an end, as also was the supply of spirits; and the pork had become distasteful to their sickly appetites. Others of the party began also to show unmistakable symptoms of scurvy. Uncertainty, if not apprehensions that a vessel of relief might not arrive, gradually took possession of the most hopeful. The turbulence of the weather, which in violence now exceeded all within their former experience, added to the horrors of their situation. Yet still they looked these terrors in the face, and by patience and faith half disarmed them. They were now so fortunate as occasionally to obtain fish, so as to preserve their stores a little longer. Sometimes they were able to catch a shag or penguin, and once Captain Gardiner and Mr. Maidment succeeded in killing a fox, and though repulsive to their feelings, the body of the animal was roasted and eaten. They saw some guanacos, which brought the loss of their powder keenly to their minds. The events of this month were few, but full of painful interest. Williams and Badcock slept at one compartment of the *Speedwell*, Erwin and Bryant occupied the other. Gardiner, Maidment, and Pearce, retired to the *Pioneer*, which was roofed over with the tent. In the second week in April, Bryant began to sicken; but he never seems to have been quite laid up. A few days later, a fearful storm raged with terrific violence, howling and crashing among the trees, bending down the tent of the *Pioneer* like a bow in the hands of a strong man, and tightening, with straining jerks, the hawser which connected the *Speedwell* with the shore. Early in the night, Gardiner, Maidment, and Pearce were driven from the *Pioneer*, and tried to enter the cavern for greater security. They only succeeded with great difficulty, as the waves dashed over the rock at the entrance. There, fearing for the safety of their friends in the *Speedwell*, they knelt down and committed them to the protecting hand of God. The angry wind still swept along. Several trees were blown down; one fell near the wreck of the *Pioneer*, just as its inmates were passing by. As soon as it was possible, after the storm, the *Speedwell* was removed higher up the Bay, and anchored at the entrance of Cook's River. The *Pioneer*, not being in a condition to be floated, remained where it was first stranded; there was therefore a considerable distance between the boats, and it was thought better for Pearce to stay with the *Speedwell*, that he might help to wait on the sick men. They looked in vain for the vessel which should relieve them, and hope began to die out. On the 21st of April, their principal supplies failing, it was necessary to put all who were in health on short allowance. At such a moment of anxiety they read and loved the Scriptures. Their poor abode was a very Bethel to their souls, for there they united in thanksgiving and prayer.

We make an extract here from Gardiner's diary. "Pioneer Cavern, May 8, 1851. Though I walk in the midst of trouble, thou wilt revive me. Mine eyes are unto thee, O God the Lord. In thee is my trust. Ps. cxxxviii. 7; and cxli. 8.

Sweet peace have they, whose minds are stayed
Firm on the Rock, in Zion laid:
No anxious cares disturb their rest.
Whate'er of earthly ills betide,
Amid the storm secure they ride,
Their souls in patience are possessed.

Children of Him, whose watchful eye
Regards the ravens when they cry,
Why need they fear impending ill?
They know their hairs are numbered all,
Nor can the smallest sparrow fall
Without their Father's sovereign will.

Though all around be dark and drear,
Nor sun, nor moon, nor stars appear
And every earthly Cherith dries;
Faith bears the drooping spirit up,
And sweetens every bitter cup,
A bow in every cloud descries.

The Lord, who gave, may surely take,
The bruised reed he will not break,
  He knows we are but dust.
The oil and meal alike may fail,
The whelming storm may long prevail,
  Yet on his promise we will trust.

Whate'er in wisdom he denies,
A richer boon his grace supplies—
  A peace the world can ne'er bestow.
Though nought remain, we're not bereft,
What most we value, still is left,—
  The Rock, whence living waters flow.

Then come what may, we'll humbly wait,
His arm was never bared too late,
  The promise will not, cannot fail.
Though dark the night, the morn will break,
His own the Lord will not forsake:
  The prayer of faith shall yet prevail;
And we shall deem the trial sweet,
That laid us waiting at his feet."

About this time Mr. Williams, although feeling, as he said, "the prostration of death upon him," writes, "To-day, May 7, we are in the highest severity of a Fuegian winter;—I suffer intense pain;—the water from the roof of the boat lodges in pools upon my bed, and all our clothes are wringing wet. Some new symptoms now show the inroads of the disease upon my system, and strongly point out to a fatal termination. Can I be in any way disappointed at this, instead of a life of much service and glory to God? No, I am not disappointed; for God's glory can only be enhanced by fulfilling the counsels of his own will; and to suffer his blessed will as much glorifies my God as to do it."

Although sick, and all around them was dreary, they set apart a day for special prayer in behalf of the sick, and for the arrival of the expected vessel. The weather was cold, and the wind blustering. At the end of May they had another fearful night. The tide and surf dashed violently. The net was broken by the strength of the tide. The wreck of the *Pioneer* was moved by the waves, and the spray dashed in. Snow was falling, and there was ice on the river. But the never-failing word of God was at hand, and amid all these distressful occurrences, it proved their best treasure, for from it Gardiner read, to his own comfort and that of his brothers in affliction. "Wait on the Lord, be of good courage, and he shall strengthen thine heart. Wait I say on the Lord." Ps. xxvii. 14. These words were entered in the diary; and, under them, the following lines:—

In heaven, the Christian pilgrim's rest,
Where all are holy, all are bless'd,
    There is no night:
No sun nor moon could add one ray
To that effulgent, endless day,
    Where all is bright,
And saints behold, with open face,
The glories of redeeming grace.

And why should there be night below,
Even in this world of sin and woe,
    Where Christians dwell?

When Egypt felt that darksome night,
In Goshen all was clear and bright,
And joy could swell
From grateful hearts, securely kept,
When judgments all around them swept.

Let that sweet word our spirits cheer,
Which quelled the tossed disciples' fear,
"Be not afraid:"
He, who could bid the tempest cease,
Can keep our souls in perfect peace,
If on him stayed:
And we shall own, 'twas good to wait,
No blessing ever came too late.

Pioneer Cavern, June 4, 1851."

Until this time, Mr. Williams hoped that, should the expected ship arrive, his disease might yield to the influence of proper treatment and good food, but on trying with the aid of Bryant to walk, he found he had no power over his limbs. But although he now gave up all hope of recovery, his mind never participated in his bodily prostration, and he kept his journal up to June 21, the shortest day of these regions, when the night lasts sixteen hours. This personal narrative he no doubt intended as a messenger to tell his Burslem friends how it fared with him in the last stage of his pilgrimage. Eventually, therefore, we believe that it was chiefly for their sakes that, by the light of a candle, and with "aching fingers," as he lay in his cheerless cabin, he continued to record the incidents and impressions of these lonely days, until the last entry was made, which contains expressions that would indicate that the mind of the writer had begun to wander. But even amidst those confused perceptions, it shows that his faith in God was still clear and unclouded.

Captain Gardiner and Mr. Maidment continued to lodge at the cavern, about a mile and a half from the mouth of Cook's River, where the boat containing the rest of the party was moored. And though the distance was not great, so exhausted and weakened were they all, that they could not maintain a daily communication. On Saturday, June 28, 1851, Gardiner's birthday, he visited the *Speedwell,* and found Mr. Williams and Badcock very ill—the shadow of death evidently creeping over the latter, who was most patient, and leaning only upon his God. On his return to his cavern, he uttered a most solemn prayer, and made a long entry in his journal:—

"We are now, by the providence of God, brought into circumstances which to the flesh are trying. . . . . But I will not be anxious on that account; we are in the Lord's service, and he is merciful and full of compassion. Though he cause grief, he will have compassion, according to the multitude of his mercies. I know that it is written, 'They that seek the Lord shall want no manner of thing that is good.' Ps. xxxiv. 10. And again, 'Cast thy burden upon the Lord, and he shall sustain thee.' Ps. lv. 22. . . . . Whatever the Lord may, in his providence, see fit to take away, it is that which he himself has bestowed. . . . . Still I pray that, if it be consistent with thy righteous will, O my heavenly Father, thou wouldst look down with compassion upon me and upon my companions, who are straitened for lack of food, and vouchsafe to provide that which is needful . . . . but, if otherwise, thy will be done. . . . . May I learn entire submission of my will to thine; may every high place of pride be abased in my heart. . . . . Lord, I pray that thou mayest be honoured in me, whether by life or by death, and that I may never depart from thee. Uphold me by thy grace, and keep me from anxious care, from murmuring, and unbelief; and may the sincere language of my heart be, under every circumstance, 'The Lord gave;' and should the Lord my God see fit to recall any of his gifts, and even to take away all, still 'blessed be the name of the Lord.' 'He hath done all things well.' One more petition I would offer to thy throne of grace, O merciful Lord; I pray that thou wouldst graciously prepare a way for the entrance of thy servants among the poor heathen of these islands. . . . . Grant, O Lord, that we may be instrumental in commencing this great and blessed work; but shouldst thou see fit, in thy providence to hedge up our way, and that we should even languish and die here, I beseech thee to raise up others, and to send forth labourers into this harvest. Let it be seen, for the manifestation of thy glory and grace, that nothing is too hard for thee . . . . and hasten the day, when the knowledge of the Lord Jesus Christ shall be manifested, not here only, but throughout every nation, and people, and tribe: and prayer and praise shall ascend, and a pure offering from the hearts of multitudes who are now sitting in darkness. . . .

"PIONEER CAVERN, *June* 28, 1851,
"(my birthday)."

At eleven o'clock on that same evening John Badcock died. He requested Mr. Williams to join him in singing a hymn. Cheerfully they sang together:—

"Arise, my soul, arise!
Shake off thy guilty fears!
The bleeding sacrifice
In my behalf appears.
Before the throne my Surety stands;
My name is written on his hands."

In a few minutes after he ceased to breathe, and the next day his remains were interred on the neighbouring bank.

Thus the first break was made in the little band of pioneers in a noble cause, and it seemed as if their bond of affection was by it only drawn the closer. They now began to realize the frightful prospect of famine unrelieved, and Gardiner's view of the terrible prospect is vividly marked by the following entry in his journal: "Be merciful unto me, O God, be merciful unto me, for my soul trusteth in thee; yea, in the shadow of thy wings will I make my refuge, until these calamities are overpast. Ps. lvii. 1." And now sustained by the most vivid faith, the stronger tenderly nursed the weak, and exerted their own failing powers to provide fresh food by every resource of ingenuity. They mended the broken net and again set it, but the floating blocks of ice tore it to pieces.

"Thus," wrote Gardiner, "the Lord has seen fit to render another means abortive, doubtless to make His power more apparent, and to show us that all our help is to come immediately from him." The next song is a march of triumph, and is headed with the words of Scripture, "The night is far spent, the day is at hand." Rom. xiii. 12. "Let us run with patience the race that is set before us, looking unto Jesus, the author and finisher of our faith." Heb. xii. 1, 2.

"Pilgrims to the heavenly land,
  Journeying through the wilderness,
Meet with snares on every hand;
  Subtle foes around them press,
Crosses still their path attend,
Till they reach their journey's end.

Till the night of toil is past,
  Storms and trials mark the way;
But we hope to reach at last
  Those bright realms of endless day,
Where ransomed saints His face adore,
Who all their sins and sorrows bore.

Forward, then! with joy we'll praise,
  Faint and weary, yet pursuing.
Each conflict o'er, the journey's less;
  A smoother path might prove our ruin.
Trials make the promise sweet,
Bring us to the mercy-seat.

How few the ills we're called to meet!
  How light the burden we sustain!
Grace makes the bitterest trial sweet,
  And turns our losses into gain.
Faith can unveil the darkest sky,
And view the heavenly Shepherd nigh.

Upheld by everlasting arms,
  Confiding souls can never sink,
Safe in the Ark, no storm alarms;
  Or, if they stand on Jordan's brink,
And Satan *there* should still pursue,
Jesus will bear them safely through.

Then let us gird our loins afresh,
  And lean upon our heavenly Guide.
We trust not in an arm of flesh,
  The Lord, our banner, will provide;
And every trial that we meet,
Shall bind us closer to his feet.

And when we reach that happy shore,
  And in Emmanuel's presence stand,
We shall confess, if not before,
  All was in love and wisdom planned;
And had one chastisement been spared,
One blessing less our souls had shared.

PIONEER CAVERN, *June* 10, 1851.

Erwin was the next who was taken ill. Mr. Williams writes, "All hands are now sadly affected. Captain Gardiner, a miracle of constitutional vigour, has suffered the least. He says he is 'none the worse, but his countenance bespeaks the contrary.'"

A very little of the original flask and a half of powder was now left. On two occasions, five ducks were killed with a single shot, so thickly were the birds settled on the water.

Again Gardiner writes:—

"They shall not be ashamed that wait for me." Isa. xlix. 23.

"He will regard the prayer of the destitute, and not despise their prayer." Ps. cii. 17.

"They that seek the Lord shall not want any good thing." Ps. xxxiv. 10.

As their thoughts fly heavenward, the poetic notes mount higher:—

"Courage, comrades, onward press,
  Let not fleeting storms offend;
We must cross the wilderness,
  Ere we reach the journey's end.
Before us lies that blissful shore,
Where sin and grief assail no more.

There is no path so rough, so drear,
  No thorny wilderness so dry,
But living streams are flowing near,
  And One to guide our footsteps nigh;
'Tis unbelief alone, that hides
The blessings, which our God provides.

Oft in affliction's darkest night,
  When all our earthly gourds decay,
The spirit takes her loftiest flight,
  And soars to realms of endless day.
In that pure light she sits serene,
And calmly views the troubled scene.

For 'tis our privilege to know,
  Whate'er of sufferings we may share,
A Father's hand inflicts the blow;
  'Tis but the children's mark we bear.

Take courage, then—the journey's short,
  These light afflictions soon will end;
By grace thus far we have been brought,
  And grace will still our steps attend."

PIONEER CAVERN, *June* 16, 1851.

On the 30th of June, Captain Gardiner and Mr. Maidment were driven from their cavern by the advancing tide. They at first retired to their sleeping boat; but as the tide threatened to sweep it away, they proceeded higher still, to a favourite rock, and there offered prayer and thanksgiving to God. The tide still advanced, and drove them from this refuge into the wood. There was no shelter there, for the drippings from the trees were worse than the rain which was falling. It was with great difficulty that they found their way to the *Speedwell.* The faithful Erwin insisted on giving up his bed to the man whom he loved to serve, and sat up with Bryant all night. When the tide permitted, Gardiner and Maidment returned to their boat in Earnest Cove, and united in prayer and thanks for their merciful preservation. They had now been seven weeks on short allowance. The provisions had been divided according to the number of persons. The store at Pioneer Cavern consisted of half a duck, one pound of salt pork, one pound of damaged tea, one pint of rice, two cakes of chocolate, four pints of peas, and six mice. From this time forward, to the end of their tragic history, all the party fed in great measure on mussels and limpets, a kind of gelatinous seaweed, and wild celery, which Mr. Maidment, although greatly debilitated, was indefatigable in collecting. In noting down their wants and difficulties at this time, Gardiner expresses his thankfulness for the grace bestowed on his suffering companions, "who, with the utmost cheerfulness, endure all without a murmur, patiently waiting the Lord's time to deliver them, or ready to languish and die here, knowing that what he shall appoint will be well."

It would appear, that about this time a hand was painted on a rock pointing to the cavern, with "Ps. lxii. 5–8," under it. The following are the words of the passage referred to, "My soul, wait thou only upon God; for my expectation is from him. He only is my rock and my salvation: he is my defence; I shall not be moved. In God is my salvation and my glory: the rock of my strength and my refuge is in God. Trust in him at all times; ye people, pour out your hearts before him: God is a refuge for us."

At the end of the month of July, Gardiner was much encouraged to hope that the health of the party at Cook's River was so much better as to present a prospect of restoration. Mr. Williams and all had partaken of celery, which the Captain had recommended, and its beneficial effects, particularly on the young surgeon, were plainly apparent. Erwin considered himself entirely free from the effects of the scurvy. Bryant was better. Pearce was weak, but both Bryant and he were about, and able to collect mussels and fuel. Still, however, days would sometimes pass without any intercourse between the inmates of the Cavern and the *Speedwell*, for the brave Gardiner was also beginning to succumb to the stern demands of famine. With what longing eyes did they scan the horizon, in hopes of descrying a sail, but nothing save a dreary tract of ocean met their view! They now suspended a table-cloth to the branch of a tree, as a signal flag, hoping to attract the attention of some passing vessel. Gardiner, although now at times obliged to keep his bed, still continued to write in his journal, from which we shall only make one extract. It is a prayer. "Let not this mission fail, though we should not be permitted to labour in it; but graciously raise up other labourers, who may convey the saving truths of thy gospel to the poor blind heathen around us."

About the 21st of August, Pearce went to Gardiner's Cavern, bearing the sad tidings that Joseph

Erwin was fast failing, and had not spoken since the previous day. Mr. Williams considered him beyond the power of human aid. On Saturday the 23d he died, and the following Tuesday terminated the sufferings of another of the boatmen, John Bryant. So one and another of this little missionary band was gathered by the Good Shepherd to a better inheritance, and higher and more glorious employments. Bryant had for a long time been failing, but no peculiar prostration marked the day of his death. No one was with him at the time; he was found dead in his berth. Captain Gardiner was now confined to his bed. Pearce was so overwhelmed with affliction at the loss of the brothers of his adoption, that he could offer little assistance. Captain Gardiner was incapable of making the least exertion, and Mr. Maidment was so exhausted by the fatigue of burying his companions, that he never recovered.

Alone in his "boat dormitory," Gardiner, now fully assured of what would be his fate, wrote, on August 27th, a farewell letter to his son. It is dated *Earnest Cove, Terra del Fuego, August* 27, 1851, and begins,—

"The Lord in his providence is taking one and another of our little missionary band unto himself, and I know not how soon he may call me, through his abounding grace and redeeming love, to join the company of the saints above, where there are pleasures for evermore. It is my desire, therefore, to prepare this letter for you, that you may have the latest proof of my affection for you, and earnest desire for your temporal and spiritual welfare. . . Should it please the Lord to incline your heart to give yourself to the gospel ministry, next to the Scriptures and devotional books, make Greek and Hebrew your principal studies: the latter should on no account be omitted. Botany is a very useful and pleasing study; should you ever go abroad, an acquaintance with plants and their properties will be of great use. So also some knowledge of medicine. . . . The next point is your profession, and the time is now arrived when this should be determined. It is of too great moment to be decided upon hastily; it will be the turning-point of your life, and your future happiness will mainly depend upon the selection which you make. Beware of following your own natural inclinations too closely. There is but one method of coming to a satisfactory conclusion. Spread the whole matter like Hezekiah before the Lord: ask counsel of him, and lean not to your own understanding; and sooner or later you will, if you ask in simple reliance on his teaching and guidance, find a way opened before you. When this has been at length decided, then take the same course with regard to the particular sphere which you devote yourself to. But I would affectionately give you this caution—Do not think of entering the gospel ministry, unless you conscientiously feel that you are constrained by the love of Christ, and the sincere desire of winning souls to him. . . . Your grandfather gave me this injunction, and I repeat it to you, 'Lead a useful life,' and I will add, take the word of God as your guide, and consult it diligently, with prayer to the Holy Spirit to open your understanding; for it is not the mere knowledge of its contents, however enlarged, critical, or clear, that will carry you safely through the snares and temptations of this evil world, but when it is received as the sincere milk of the Word, by which our souls are daily nourished and strengthened: then and then only, we grow thereby, and are prepared for the cares and trials of life, and are renewed in the inward man: thus we are enabled to adorn the doctrine we profess, and become gradually meet for that incorruptible and undefiled inheritance that fadeth not away, reserved for all those who live by faith on the Lord Jesus Christ."

On the 28th, he wrote a letter to his daughter, in which he took a tender farewell of her, and gave her his fatherly counsel. On the 29th, he wrote his last letter to his wife, from which we present the following extract: "If I have a wish for the good of my fellow-men, it is that the Terra del Fuego Mission might be prosecuted with vigour, and the work in South America, more especially the Chilidugu branch."

On the 30th of August, Captain Gardiner made an attempt to leave the cavern, and take up his quarters in the boat; but finding him unable to walk without crutches, Mr. Maidment (with no slight exertion in his weak state) cut a pair of forked sticks, which might have answered the purpose had Gardiner had strength enough to proceed. But he found himself utterly unable, and after proceeding a very short distance, was obliged to return. From Monday the 1st of September, until the 5th, the date of his last communication, it is probable that he employed himself in revising the memoranda which bore the heading, "*Missionary Memoranda*, 1851," afterwards brought to England by Captain Morshead.

Mr. Maidment retained his energy and consideration to the last. On the 2d of September he left the boat, but was unable to return, and his remains were found in Pioneer Cavern.

From this time Captain Gardiner was alone. On the same day, when dreading the pangs of thirst, he prayed for strength to procure water, and found himself able to get out, and collect a little in his India rubber shoe, upon which he makes the pious remark, "With what mercies my heavenly Father loads me! Blessed be his holy name!" On the 3d of September he made this entry in his journal: "Blessed be my heavenly Father for all the comforts I enjoy:—a comfortable bed, no pain, not even the gnawings of hunger. I am so weak that I can scarcely turn on my couch, but through God's abounding grace, I am kept in perfect peace, refreshed by a sense of the love of Christ, and by the assurance that he orders all things in wisdom and mercy. I cast all my cares upon him, waiting for him to dispose of me according to his pleasure. If I am in him, it matters not whether I live or die. I commit to him my body and soul, begging him to take my dear wife and children under the shadow of his wings. May he comfort and keep them, strengthen and sanctify them, that we may celebrate together, in a better world, his love in redeeming us with his precious blood." On the 5th of Sept. 1851, being reduced nearly to the last extremity, he wrote, "Great and marvellous are the loving-kindnesses of the Lord! For four days I have taken no food, but he has preserved me from feeling the pangs of hunger and thirst."

The following letter, addressed to the young surgeon, whom it never reached, contains the last words of Allen Gardiner. It was found on the shore, discoloured by exposure, and torn. It was written in pencil, partly full and partly in a fragmentary manner. The following is thought to be the correct reading:—"My dear Mr. Williams. The Lord has seen fit to call home another of our little company. Our dear departed brother left the boat on Tuesday at noon, and he has not since returned. Doubtless he is in the presence of his Redeemer, whom he served so faithfully. Yet a little while, and through grace we may join that blessed throng to sing the praises of Christ throughout eternity. I neither hunger nor thirst, though five days without food!

Marvellous loving-kindness to me a sinner! Your affectionate brother in Christ, Allen F. Gardiner. Sept. 6, 1851."

Thus, far from their homes and friends, perished this little band—the Pioneers of Fuegia. "Blessed are the dead which die in the Lord; yea, saith the Spirit, that they may rest from their labours; and their works do follow them. They hunger no more, neither thirst any more, for the Lamb which is in the midst of the throne doth feed them." Rev. xiv. 12, 13; vii. 16, 17. What needed they of hearse and funeral equipment? Did not

> "The wild winds ring their funeral knell,
> Sweetly as solemn peal of pious passing bell?"

* * * * * * *

There lay those precious relics, the diaries and memoranda, on which were impressed the inner thoughts of hearts devoted to Jesus Christ. There lay the tender, farewell letters of a loving, dying father and husband. The tide ebbed and flowed, but injured not these fragile memorials of Christian martyrs. The spray dashed over them, and left indelible stains, but the handwriting is still plain in almost all instances. The rain poured down from above. The winds blew loud and strong, but a sleepless eye watched over them, an almighty hand protected them. Twenty days after the death of Captain Gardiner, a schooner, the *John Davison*, sailed from Monte Video, by orders from Mr. Lafone, to assist the mission party. Twice before he had made arrangements for vessels to touch at Picton Island; in January, and in June or July. The first vessel was wrecked, and the second acted contrary to his express instructions. As soon as he discovered this failure, Mr. Lafone, in great anxiety, dispatched the *John Davison*, Captain Smyley, on a special voyage. This vessel, after saving the crew of a Danish barque, who had been cast away on Staten Island thirty-one days before, and were then starving, anchored on the 21st of October at Banner Cove. The directions painted on the rocks were plain, 'Gone to Spaniard's Harbour." The bottles were dug up, and the letters read. Captain Smyley therefore steered to Spaniard's Harbour, and found the *Speedwell* on the beach, containing a dead body, probably that of Mr. Williams, as it is not likely that after having been so long confined to his bed, he should have been able to leave it. On shore lay the remains of another, supposed to be that of Pearce; and there can be little doubt that he was the last survivor of the party. The Indians, whose naked foot-prints were observed on the strand, had most likely found him still alive and had murdered him. A grave was near; and books, papers, medicine, everything which was of no value to the savages, were found scattered on the deck or strewn along the beach.

Captain Smyley writes: "The two captains and the stout-hearted seamen who went with me wept like children at the sight. With boats unfit to take them to the Falklands, having no resting-place, for they were driven from point to point by the Indians; always in dread and fear; add to these the stormy, dreary, long nights, with almost perpetual ice and snow; and cooped up in a small boat, so laden that there was scarce room to move; without food, and afflicted with that terrible disease, the scurvy; and their situation can be judged. of partly." Captain Smyley had barely time to bury the body found on shore, when a violent gale arose and drove him from his anchorage and out to sea. His little vessel, laden with the crew of the cast-away barque, could prosecute the search no further, but was forced to return to Monte Video.

Before this terrible news reached England, H. M. S. *Dido*, under Captain Morshead, left the Falklands on January 6, 1852, and arrived at Banner Cove on the 19th. They sought in vain for the bottles under the direction-posts, unconscious that they had been removed by Captain Smyley. But the directions painted on the rocks, induced them to go to Spaniard's Harbour, where their notice was attracted by a boat lying on the beach. As there was every indication of a gale, and the Captain was anxious to get the ship to sea in safety for the night, he sent two of his party to reconnoitre and return immediately. They came back shortly, bringing some books and papers, having discovered the bodies of Captain Gardiner and Mr. Maidment unburied. On one of the papers was written legibly, but without a date, "If you walk along the beach for a mile and a half you will find us in the other boat, hauled up in the mouth of the river. Delay not, we are starving." After hearing this sad intelligence, it was impossible to leave; and next morning, amidst threatening weather, Captain Morshead landed. Mr. Maidment's body lay in the cavern where he had so often spent the night, and in which the stores rescued from the *Pioneer* were kept. Outside on the rocks was painted, by way of direction to any visitor, a hand, and under it Ps. lxii. 5—8. Captain Gardiner's body was lying beside the wreck of the *Pioneer.* It seemed he had left his berth, but being too weak to climb in again, he had died at the side of the boat. The remains were collected together and buried close to the spot. The funeral service was read; an inscription was placed on the rocks near his own text; three volleys of musketry, the only tribute of respect they could pay to the memory of this lofty-minded man and his devoted companions, who have perished in the cause of the gospel, were fired; the ship's colours were struck half-mast high, and having fulfilled her mournful commission, the *Dido* went on her way.

And now, dear Christian readers, let none imagine that the labours of Gardiner and his companions perished with them. They have not died in vain, for the echo of their sufferings, patience, and happiness in death, has found its way to the hearts of many thousands, and claim an equal sympathy with those of the noble Franklin and his gallant crew. Are men only great because of success? Is it only the "conquering hero that is taken to the world's heart?" Is true heroism and virtue reckoned only by results? Can we read such lives as those of Sir Hugh Willoughby, frozen to death, with all his crew, in the icy waste of Lapland; Franklin, brave and tender-hearted Franklin, whose ship was called a paradise; Bellot, the gallant young Frenchman, whose untimely death brought tears to the eyes of the stern old sailors, his ship-mates; our own Kane, too, who—

"With a rocky purpose in his soul,
Breasted the gathering snows,
Clung to the drifting floes,
By want beleagured, and by winter chased,
Seeking the brother lost amid that frozen waste;"—

can we read those lives and ask, "What use?" And what is the moral of these lives? Not "glory," but "duty," was their motive, as it also was that of our Patagonian missionaries, whose whole testimony goes to show their devotion in the greatest cause that man is called to aid. What use was a mission to Fuegia? May not much be learned from the lessons taught by the sufferings and the self-sacrifice of these missionary martyrs; how no Christian need fear that his circumstances will be ever so forlorn, but that the Comforter can still inspire him with a joy unspeakable and full of glory. Illumined by an immortal prospect, the dreary cabin becomes "none other than the gate of heaven," and cheered by a celestial visitor, the long hours of an antarctic night are never counted. Famishing for want of food, they are, nevertheless, happy in being counted worthy to suffer for Christ's sake; and when in their little hospital, the first death takes place, the Christian soldier asks his feeble companion to join him in a hymn of praise.

CHAPTER XX.

THE FLOATING MONUMENT.

"We see but dimly through the mists and vapours;
  Amid these earthly damps,
What seem to us but sad funereal tapers,
  May be heaven's distant lamps."

When the fate of Captain Gardiner and his companions became known in England, it aroused the most opposite feelings among the people,—pity, admiration, blame, grief, thankfulness, indignation. Those who recognized no claim upon Christians to carry the gospel to the uncivilized heathen, pronounced this effort and all such to be absurd, chimerical folly. Others who could admire the deeds of those brave men who lay down their lives at their country's call, or sacrifice themselves at the claims of humanity, could see nothing to praise in the devotion of those seven men who gave up all for Christ and his cause. An indignant outcry was raised against the promoters of this enterprise, which was condemned as a foolish and prodigal waste of life. These censures were replied to by other journalists in a more humane and elevated tone. They indeed reproved those who supported Captain Gardiner, for their want of commercial knowledge. But the memory of the seven brave pioneers was treated with respect, as a sacred treasure not to be profaned by the touch of unsympathizing criticism. Meanwhile, the echo of their sufferings, patience, and happiness in death, found its way to the hearts of many thousands throughout the country, both rich and poor. Some were roused to seek a closer acquaintance with the gracious Saviour, who had so wonderfully made his cheering presence felt, by his suffering servants. Some with tears lamented their own lukewarmness, and made a solemn surrender of themselves to the Lord's service in their several stations of life. Some were arrested in a career of worldly excitement or hollow profession of religion, by the voice of God, speaking to them from the graves of Tierra del Fuego. If such alone were the result of the mission, it was said, "They have not died in vain."

But the great question still demanded a reply, "Was the mission to Patagonia and Fuegia to be abandoned?" Those who had most loudly condemned the promoters of the mission, supported their own view, by calling the attempt an "unadvised" one. It was desirable, therefore, to take the advice of those who were best acquainted with the localities.

Captain Morshead, who had visited the spot, and

witnessed the dreadful scene of sorrow, and brought home the journals and relics from Spaniard Harbour, said, "There would be no doubt as to the ultimate success of a mission here." Again, writing to the Rev. G. Pakenham Despard, the Honorary Secretary of the Patagonian Missionary Society, Captain Morshead says, "As for Captain Gardiner, and his party, none should grieve over them; for their sufferings are over, and they are enjoying a brighter and a happier world in the presence of Him whom they served so faithfully. I can only say, *I trust neither yourself nor the Society will be discouraged from following up to the utmost the cause in which you have embarked: and ultimate success is as certain as the present degraded state of the natives is evident. Their state is a perfect discredit to the age we live in, within a few hundred miles of an English colony.*"

On the receipt of this letter, Mr. Despard at once published to the world his resolve in the following words, "WITH GOD'S HELP, THE MISSION TO TIERRA DEL FUEGO, SHALL BE MAINTAINED." When this resolution had been taken, the missionary memoranda of Captain Gardiner were carefully studied, together with the plan which he there proposed for the future prosecution of the mission. While this plan was being considered, two communications were made to Mr. Despard, the one by Captain B. J. Sulivan, R.N., who had just returned from the Falklands, where he had been acting as naval surveyor, the other by Mr. Lafone of Monte Video, whose attempts to relieve Captain Gardiner have been already related. The three suggestions which were now before the committee were so nearly identical, that the similarity was quite remarkable. The plan decided on was to take up ground on one of the Falkland Islands, and *from thence to hold a cautious intercourse with the Feugians, by means of a schooner to be named the* Allen Gardiner. This schooner would thus be both a *floating monument* to the memory of the departed, and the means of carrying forward the work he commenced.

It was still thought desirable to submit the plan to Captain FitzRoy, R.N., the commander of the *Beagle*, when engaged in the survey of the coasts of Patagonia and Tierra del Fuego. The following is an extract from his reply: "It appears to me that your present plan is practicable, and comparatively safe; that it offers a fairer prospect of success than most missionary enterprises at their commencement, and that it would be difficult to suggest one less objectionable."

One more witness must be brought forward. It may be remembered, that when the *John Davison* sailed from Monte Video, to convey assistance to Captain Gardiner, Captain Nichols sailed in her as a volunteer. He was a man of thoroughly practical acquaintance with the navigation of those seas. Mr. Despard received the following communication from him: "Your mission, if properly conducted,

I conceive practicable, and eminently desirable. I should certainly recommend the vessel to be well armed, and from 100 to 150 tons, rigged American fashion, fore-and-aft-sails, no square ones; she would then be able to work off a lee shore."

Accordingly, the keel of a schooner, to be named the *Allen Gardiner*, was laid in Dartmouth dockyard on November 1, 1853. A solemn prayer was offered to God for his blessing; and the deep Amen showed that the prayer was echoed from many hearts. The *Allen Gardiner* was launched on July 11, 1854. Again a solemn service was held in the dockyard, and the vessel was consecrated as a missionary ship in the service of Jesus Christ. On the 24th of October she sailed for the Falklands, with a competent crew, and having on board Mr. Garland Phillips as catechist.

Unforeseen difficulties prevented a clergyman from accompanying the expedition, and after various disappointments, Captain Gardiner's tried and trusted friend, Mr. Despard, offered his services as superintendent. He had been, under God, the mainstay of the Society from the time of Captain Gardiner's final departure from England. Captain Gardiner's only son freely offered his best services to his father's friend; and they left England in June 1856, and arrived at Stanley, in East Falkland, on the 31st of August.

The British government allowed them to take possession of Keppel Island, which is about four miles by six, as their missionary station, and in 1859 the missionary staff was composed of the Rev. G. P. Despard, his wife and five children, besides a young man whom he had adopted and was training as a missionary; and Messrs Phillips and Schmidt, catechists. In addition to these must be named the master of the *Allen Gardiner*, Mr. Fell, who was zealously exploring the coast of the mainland and islands to determine the best points for future operations. A number of youth had been placed under the charge of Mr. Garland Phillips, some of whom had given hopeful indications of future usefulness, while Mr. Schmidt was seeking intercourse with the tribes of Patagonia. But here God again interposed to try the faith and patience of his people. While the mission ship was on the coast of Woollya, and Captain Fell, with the catechist and six of the crew on shore, they were attacked by about two hundred Fuegians, and cruelly massacred with clubs and stones. From November to April, 1860, the vessel tossed upon the bloodstained shore, when it was recovered by Captain Smyley of the *Nancy*. The damage of the schooner was not so great as might have been anticipated. Her chain had caught under a submarine rock, and so was shortened, otherwise her destruction would have been inevitable. The interior of the schooner had been ransacked, and everything capable of removal taken away by the natives, but the hull and spars were sound, and with refitting the vessel was capable of being again brought into service.

While some Christians were inclined to see in this disaster the hand of God put forth to stay the work in Tierra del Fuego, and to mark his disapprobation, Mr. Despard felt that it was only God's way of directing more attention to this difficult and dangerous undertaking. Thus the work of educating the aborigines at the station on Keppel Island is vigorously prosecuted. The son of Captain Gardiner has been recently ordained to the ministry, and has opened an entirely new mission among the Aracaunian Indians of Chili. Mr. Schmidt has been joined with Mr. Konisiker, and they are labouring with success in Patagonia. The Society are seeking openings for missionaries among the aborigines of the Brazils, La Plata, and Bolivia, and expect again to resume operations among the islands of Fuegia.

May God prosper them in their work of faith and labour of love; and may the trials and afflictions and patience of his servants redound to his glory.

THE END.

www.ingramcontent.com/pod-product-compliance
Lightning Source LLC
LaVergne TN
LVHW020239110826
845151LV00003B/976